TORONTO MEDIEVAL LATIN TEXTS 31

TORONTO MEDIEVAL LATIN TEXTS

THE SERMONS OF WILLIAM OF NEWBURGH

Edited from
Oxford, Bodleian Library, MS Rawlinson C. 31,
London, Lambeth Palace Library, MS 73,
and London, British Library, MS Stowe 62

by

A.B. KRAEBEL

Published for the
CENTRE FOR MEDIEVAL STUDIES
by the
PONTIFICAL INSTITUTE OF MEDIAEVAL STUDIES
Toronto

Library and Archives Canada Cataloguing in Publication

William, of Newburgh, 1136-1201?
The sermons of William of Newburgh : edited from Oxford, Bodleian Library, MS Rawlinson C.31, London, Lambeth Palace Library, MS 73, and London, British Library, MS Stowe 62 / by A.B. Kraebel.

(Toronto medieval Latin texts, ISSN 0082-5050 ; 31)
Text in Latin with introd. and notes in English.
Includes bibliographical references and index.
ISBN 978-0-88844-481-3

1. Catholic Church–Sermons. 2. Sermons, Latin. I. Kraebel, A.B. (Andrew Brock), 1983– II. Pontifical Institute of Mediaeval Studies III. Bodleian Library. Manuscript. Rawlinson C. 31 IV. Lambeth Palace Library. Manuscript. 73 V. British Library. Manuscript. Stowe 62 VI. Title. VII. Series: Toronto medieval Latin texts ; 31

BX1756.W535S47 2010 252'.02 C2009-903733-5

59 Queen's Park Crescent East
Toronto, Ontario, Canada M5S 2C4

Printed in Canada

PREFACE

The TORONTO MEDIEVAL LATIN TEXTS series is published for the Centre for Medieval Studies, University of Toronto, by the Pontifical Institute of Mediaeval Studies. The series provides affordable editions, generally based on a single carefully chosen manuscript, suitable for use in university-level courses in medieval Latin. In approving projects, the editorial board bears in mind the pedagogical utility of the texts proposed.

At the same time, the series also aims to further original research by publishing previously unedited texts from reliable single-manuscript versions of particular textual, historical, and codicological interest and importance, in recognition that the scribal makers of such versions were important participants in the ongoing development of the text. The manuscript is emended only to restore sense, not to reconstruct an original authorial version; the minimal textual apparatus omits variants irrelevant to the integrity of the selected manuscript. Manuscript orthography and syntax are carefully preserved.

The Editorial Board, beyond merely supervising, takes responsibility for reviewing all proposals, for examining all specimens of volume editors' work, and for final reading of all editions published. It decides on all matters of editorial policy.

As General Editor, I would like to express my gratitude to the Centre for Medieval Studies for sponsorship of the series; to the Press of the Pontifical Institute and its unfailingly cordial and astute staff, particularly Fred Unwalla; to A.G. Rigg, whose sustained and tireless work as General Editor of the series for its first thirty volumes set a daunting standard to emulate; to Anna Burko, whose care and precision as Editorial Assistant did so much to maintain the standards of the series for over thirty years; to Philippa Matheson, whose expert work as Editorial Assistant has eased my transition into the position of General Editor beginning with the present thirty-first volume of the series. Finally, I am deeply indebted to all members of the editorial board, past and present, for the generosity of their sustained involvement, without which the series could not exist.

D.T.

ACKNOWLEDGMENTS

My work on this edition began while I was a Research Fellow at the Beinecke Rare Book and Manuscript Library at Yale in 2007. I am happy to thank that institution and its director, Frank Turner, for the grant they provided to support this work. It is also a pleasure to acknowledge the particular members of the community of medievalists at Yale who provided me with invaluable guidance and support throughout the course of this project: Margot Fassler, Alastair Minnis, Roberta Frank, and James J. John, as well as many of my fellow graduate students, including Samantha Lily Katz, Colleen Farrell, Katie Bugyis, Simon Gatsby, T. Martin Verrot, Charlotte E.L. Kingston, and Michael Ellis. While they were in London, Jessica Brantley and Jane L. Carroll provided me with further information regarding the manuscripts that contain the texts of this edition. For permission to edit these texts from manuscripts in their possession, my thanks are owed to the British Library, the Bodleian Library, University of Oxford, and the Trustees of Lambeth Palace Library. David Townsend and the members of the editorial board who served as anonymous readers are owed many thanks: their criticism has greatly improved the quality of my work. Support of a different kind, though every bit as valuable, has been provided by my fiancée, Elise Dunphe, and, as has always been the case, by the rest of my family: my two brothers and my parents.

As a sign of my appreciation for the unflagging enthusiasm that they have always shown for anything I do, this book is dedicated to my mother, Janet, and my father, Richard.

A.B.K.

ABBREVIATIONS

AASS	Acta Sanctorum
Bede, *Historia*	Bede, *Historia ecclesiastica gentis Anglorum*
CAO	Hesbert, *Corpus Antiphonalium Officii*
CCCM	Corpus Christianorum, Continuatio Mediaevalis
CCSL	Corpus Christianorum, Series Latina
CSEL	Corpus Scriptorum Ecclesiasticorum Latinorum
Explanatio	see Gorman
Gorman	*William of Newburgh's Explanatio sacri epithalamii in matrem sponsi*, ed. J.C. Gorman
Hearne	*Guilielmi Neubrigensis Historia sive Chronica rerum anglicarum*, ed. Thomas Hearne
Howlett	William of Newburgh, *Historia rerum Anglicarum*, ed. R. Howlett
PL	Patrologia Latina
Stegmüller	Friedrich Stegmüller, *Repertorium Biblicum Medii Aevi*

SIGLA

R	Oxford, Bodleian Library, MS Rawlinson C. 31
L	London, Lambeth Palace Library, MS 73
S	London, British Library, MS Stowe 62

CONTENTS

INTRODUCTION

Like Bede (d. 735), the writer on whom he modelled himself, the canon regular William of Newburgh (1136–ca. 1200) is known primarily as an historian. Indeed, along with such writers as William of Malmesbury (1080/95–ca. 1143), he has come to be seen as one of the preeminent historians of England in the twelfth century.[1] The atrocities that he records following the Conquest, as well as his prodigious accounts of blood raining from the sky and green children emerging from the ground, make William's *Historia Anglorum* a vivid and rich source for English political and ecclesiastical history.[2] Yet, as is also the case with Bede, it is impossible fully to understand William apart from his identity as a member of a particular religious order. John Gillingham has called William 'by far the most religious-minded of later twelfth-century English historians,' and the late M.J. Kennedy demonstrated how readily William's major exegetical work, a Marian commentary on the Canticle of Canticles, provides a hermeneutic with which his *Historia* might be read.[3] The three sermons printed in this edition, heretofore little studied,[4] offer the opportunity for yet more refined analysis of William's interpretative and compositional priorities, including his devotion to the Virgin Mary and his understanding of allegory, the liturgy, and English

1 Nancy Partner, *Serious Entertainments: The Writing of History in Twelfth-Century England* (Chicago 1977), pp 51–52, assesses William's treatment by historians of the nineteenth and twentieth centuries.

2 Though William's history has traditionally been entitled *Historia rerum Anglicarum*, the oldest extant manuscript of the text bears the title *Historia Anglorum* (see the list of the contents of Stowe transcribed below, p. 8). For Howlett's critical edition of the *Historia* see the Select Bibliography, p. 31

3 Gillingham, 'The Historian as Judge,' p. 1275; Kennedy, 'Faith in the one God,' pp 148 ff. For other works on William's *Historia*, see the bibliography following this introduction. The Canticle-commentary has been published by J.C. Gorman; it is listed in Stegmüller, no. 3009. The only author to treat this commentary at length is Rachel Fulton, *From Judgment to Passion*, pp 297, 301–303, and, especially, 428–470; *eadem*, 'Mimetic Devotion.'

4 The sermons were printed, though uncritically and with many errors, by Thomas Hearne in 1719.

national identity. Through these texts, a clearer picture emerges of William, his life as a canon regular, and his preoccupations as a late-twelfth-century Englishman.

The three texts of this edition are identified as sermons or homilies in the manuscripts (about which, see below), and they offer William's exegesis of the liturgical verses 'Benedicamus Patrem et Filium cum Sancto Spiritu' and 'Gloria Patri et Filio et Spiritui Sancto'; his interpretation of Luke 11:27, 'Factum est autem, cum [Ihesus] hec diceret, extollens uocem quedam mulier de turba dixit illi, "Beatus uenter qui te portauit et ubera que suxisti"';[5] and his meditation upon the story of Alban, the British proto-martyr. Though he addresses very different subjects in each of these texts, William's constant, often explicitly stated purpose is to describe the life to which his monastic audience ought to aspire, using the Virgin, the angelic choirs, and Alban as distinct illustrations of the same, perfected Church. Further patterns emerge from these texts, lending coherence to the entirety of William's œuvre: the Virgin and Alban are described using similar phrases from the Canticle of Canticles, for example, following interpretations presented in William's Canticle-commentary, while William's use of Bede in his sermon on Alban likewise ties the priorities of his exegetical writing to those of the *Historia*.

In all of these texts, William demonstrates that his memory is filled with phrases from Scripture and the Fathers, gained from a lifetime spent chanting the daily round of the Office; he shows his deference to the *auctoritas* of patristic opinion, and, at the same time, his ability to use his knowledge of the Bible to refine and explore the possible range of meanings expressed in the writings of the Fathers. Before analysing the contents of his sermons, it will be useful for us to consider what can be known about their author, whose life as a member of a religious order and as a man born at the beginning of the anarchy of Stephen's reign, had a readily apparent influence on all of his literary endeavours.

5 For this and all other Scriptural quotations in the Introduction, I have followed the biblical text as it is quoted in William's sermons.

William of Newburgh

Few details survive regarding the life of William of Newburgh, called William Petit or Parvus,[6] and almost all of what can be known about the canon must be drawn from passing comments made in his *Historia* and Canticle-commentary. Regarding the date of his birth, at least, William is clear: he states that he was born within the first year of Stephen's reign, and Richard Howlett, the editor of the *Historia*, has fixed that date at 1136.[7] Another remark, regarding streams called 'Gipse' that flow 'haud procul a loco nativitatis meae,' might refer to the streams now called the Gypsey Race, which run into the sea near Bridlington, suggesting that William was born in or around that city.[8]

Regardless of where he was born, William spent most of his life with the canons regular of Newburgh Priory, roughly forty-five miles to the west of Bridlington and twenty miles north of York.[9] He states, 'Neuburgensi[s] ecclesia … me in Christo a puero aluit.'[10] Since Newburgh was a new foundation, begun during William's lifetime, we may ascertain roughly how old he must have been when he joined that community. Newburgh began with the grant of a church by Roger de Mowbray in 1142/3 to the canons at Bridlington, but the new community had to stay at Hood, just northwest of Newburgh, until Newburgh was completed in 1145. When the community resettled at the new priory, Hood was reduced to the rank of a cell.[11] William's

6 At the end of his Canticle-commentary in Brussels, Bibliothèque Royale, MS 243 (1869), William identifies himself as 'Willelmus cognomine Parvus.' Gorman, p. 364.

7 *Historia* 1. Proem (Howlett, p. 19). For Howlett's argument in favour of a date of 1136 over 1135, see Howlett, p. xviii. Other accounts of William's life include Gorman, pp 3–17, and Gransden, *Historical Writing in England*, pp 263–268.

8 *Historia* 1.28 (Howlett, p. 85). For Howlett's interpretation of this statement, see his introduction, pp xvii–xviii.

9 Howlett maintains that there is little evidence in the *Historia* to suggest that the canon travelled much beyond Yorkshire or Durham. Howlett, p. xxi.

10 *Historia* 1.15 (Howlett, p. 51).

11 David Knowles and R. Neville Hadcock, *Medieval Religious Houses, England and Wales* (New York 1972), p. 167. The charters from Roger to

specific reference to the *Neuburgensis ecclesia* would appear to preclude the possibility of his schooling by the community before it had settled in Newburgh, in which case he would have been at least nine years old when he joined them. Therefore, if his reference to his *pueritia* at Newburgh is accurate, William must have entered the community of canons not long after they had established themselves there.

From his childhood, therefore, William was involved in the life of the Newburgh community. As Howlett imagined it, 'starting as one of the children in the choir, and attracting notice by an early exhibition of the solid abilities and sober good sense which he certainly showed in later life, [William] won his way upwards and was admitted to full brotherhood through the recognition of his personal merits.'[12]

Both of William's major works, the *Historia* and Canticle-commentary, were composed at the request of the abbots of nearby Cistercian houses, and it therefore appears that William may have held some position of authority within his priory.[13] Indeed, the content of the sermons edited here, especially when considered together with William's historical writing, suggests something more specific about his later role at Newburgh than Howlett's sketch provides. For William was participating in a trend of historical writing by cathedral canons and members of religious orders in twelfth-century England, and

---

Newburgh are published in Clay, *Early Yorkshire Charters*, vol. 9, pp 244–245. On the growth of monasticism in Yorkshire in this period, see Burton, *Monastic Order in Yorkshire*. On the canons regular in England, see Thompson, *History and Architectural Description*; Dickinson, *Origins of the Austin Canons*; Herbert, 'Transformation of Hermitages,' pp 131–145.

12 Howlett, p. xx. The deed discovered by H.E. Salter, now British Library, MS Cotton Vitellius E.xv, fol. 74, believed by Salter to demonstrate that William did not join Newburgh until the 1180s, appears to have referred to a different William. Salter, 'William of Newburgh,' *English Historical Review* 22 (1907) 510–514; critiqued by Gorman, pp 11–17.

13 The *Historia* was written at the request of Ernaldus of Rievaulx (Howlett, pp 3–4), while the Canticle-commentary was written at the request of Roger of Byland (Gorman, pp 71–72). These houses were among the most influential in northern England ca. 1200.

many of these historians are known to have held the office of cantor in their communities, e.g. Eadmer of Canterbury (ca. 1060–ca. 1124),[14] Symeon of Durham (d. after 1129),[15] Hugh the Chanter of York (d. ca. 1140),[16] and William of Malmesbury.[17] Composing a history, however lengthy, was a natural extension of the responsibilities of the cantor. All cantors wrote history of a kind, recording the deaths of members and patrons of the community, so that they might be prayed for in the liturgy on the appropriate dates.[18] Further, in so far as he was charged with overseeing his community's liturgy—preparing liturgical books, assigning singers to perform specific roles, and directing complex processions—the cantor also governed the monastery's or cathedral's conception of time. Orchestrating the liturgy was itself a form of historiography: canons and monks conceptualized history largely in terms of the liturgy, marked by the major feasts, especially Easter, but also by the various lesser feasts of the saints that filled the calendar. By overseeing the celebration

14 Eadmer was studied extensively by R.W. Southern in relation to his work on Anselm of Canterbury; see especially *Saint Anselm and His Biographer: A Study of Monastic Life and Thought, 1059–ca. 1130* (Cambridge 1963); *Saint Anselm: A Portrait in a Landscape* (Cambridge 1990).

15 See the various essays collected in *Symeon of Durham: Historian of Durham and the North*, ed. D. Rollason (Stamford 1998); and *Anglo-Norman Durham, 1093–1193*, ed. D. Rollason, M. Harvey, and M. Prestwich (Woodbridge 1994).

16 Hugh was precentor at York Minster ca. 1130; see his *History of the Church of York, 1066–1127*, ed. C. Johnson, rev. M. Brett, C.N.L. Brooke, and M. Winterbottom (Oxford 1990).

17 For William's position as cantor at Malmesbury, see his *Gesta Regum Anglorum: The History of the English Kings*, ed. R.A.B. Mynors, R.M. Thomson, and M. Winterbottom (Oxford 1998), vol. 2, p. xxxviii.

18 For Lanfranc's description of the office of the cantor in England, see *The Monastic Constitutions of Lanfranc*, ed. D. Knowles, rev. C.N.L. Brooke (Oxford 2002), pp 118–122. For an example of the office of the cantor (also called the 'armarius' or librarian) described in an Augustinian customary, see the *Liber ordinis Sancti Victoris Parisiensis*, ed. L. Jocqué and L. Milis, CCCM 61 (Turnhout 1984), pp 78–86. The changing responsibilities of the cantor throughout the Middle Ages are described by Fassler, 'The Office of the Cantor,' pp 29–51. See also David Knowles, *The Monastic Order in England*, 2nd ed. (Cambridge 1963), pp 428–430.

of these feasts, the cantor shaped his community's sense of history.[19]

That William was the cantor of Newburgh is supported by the content of the texts edited here. As we will see, in his first sermon, William exhorts his monastic audience to recall that their liturgical performance brings them into a relationship with the angels, who praise God with their own songs in heaven. The Trinitarian songs of the liturgy, he writes, are not only sung aloud in choir, but they also resound in the 'guttur mentis' when one meditates, and they are similarly apparent in the community's 'conuersatio' or monastic way of life. This focus on the liturgy, especially on liturgical song and its use as a metaphor for a proper Christian life, suggests that the author was a cantor, reflecting on the liturgy that he oversaw.[20] Though further manuscript evidence will have to come to light before any certain conclusions can be reached, the functions of the office of the cantor in the twelfth century and the content of William's writings make it very likely that he was Newburgh's cantor in the 1190s.

Like so many other details of his life, the date of William's death is unclear. The fifth book of the *Historia* breaks off suddenly, as the canon relates events of late 1197, with only one additional event from mid-1198 noted, suggesting that William had soon thereafter fallen into poor health, and his subsequent death prevented the completion of his historiographical project.[21] Of course, William's omission of events after 1198 does not indicate that he had died before those events took place, but only that he did not record them.[22] However, it seems likely that if he were alive and had learned of the major events

19 The idea of the liturgy shaping a sense of history is explored in Margot Fassler, *The Virgin of Chartres: Making History through Liturgy and the Arts* (New Haven, forthcoming); see also Susan Boynton, *Shaping a Monastic Identity: Liturgy and History at the Imperial Abbey of Farfa, 1000–1125* (Ithaca 2006).

20 For the relationship between the cantor and the liturgy discussed in similar terms, see Fassler, *Gothic Song*, pp 38–57.

21 Howlett, pp xxiii–xxiv; Gillingham, 'William of Newburgh and Emperor Henry VI,' pp 68–70.

22 Such was the argument of Kate Norgate, 'William of Newburgh,' *Dictionary of National Biography* 61 (1900) 360–363; *eadem*, 'The Date of

of the following years, such as the death of Richard I and the coronation of John in 1199, William would have included such happenings in his *Historia*. The date of William's death, therefore, though no more than an approximation, must be set ca. 1200.

The Sermons

The texts printed in this edition are found immediately after the *Historia Anglorum* in the two oldest extant manuscripts of that work, London, British Library, MS Stowe 62 (S) and London, Lambeth Palace Library, MS 73 (L). The first two texts, though with their order reversed, are also found in Oxford, Bodleian Library, MS Rawlinson C. 31 (R; descriptions of all three manuscripts may be found below).[23] William's authorship of these pieces is noted explicitly in Lambeth, wherein the scribe labels the second and third texts, 'item tractatus eiusdem ad eundem,' (fols 110r and 115v), indicating that the Lambeth scribe believed William, the author of the *Historia*, to be the author of these three works as well.[24] While there is no such attribution in Rawlinson or Stowe, the uniformity of the latter's execution, discussed below, supports the ascription made by the Lambeth scribe. This attribution is supported further by

---

Composition of William of Newburgh's History,' *English Historical Review* 19 (1904) 288–297.

23 Because Rawlinson has served as the base manuscript for the texts it contains, the order of William's sermons in this edition follows Rawlinson, not Lambeth and Stowe.

24 Though William's authorship of these texts is supported by the execution of Stowe, discussed below, the import of the phrase 'ad eundem' is not. By stating that the texts were written 'to the same,' the Lambeth scribe is suggesting that these sermons were addressed to Abbot Ernaldus of Rievaulx, the dedicatee of the *Historia*. However, William makes no reference to these shorter texts in the dedicatory epistle that prefaces the *Historia* (Howlett, pp 3–4), and so their intended audience is unclear. While William could have composed them with a Cistercian audience in mind, it is also very likely that they are based at least in part on sermons William delivered to his own community of canons. This latter hypothesis is supported by the sermons' circulation in Rawlinson, independent of the *Historia*.

the close relationship that exists between William's Canticle-commentary and his homily on Lc 11:27 (see below).

Though the texts do not bear titles on the folios on which they begin, these can be supplied from a table of contents written in the same hand as the body text on fol. 2v of Stowe:

Liber Sancte Marie de Nouoburgo,
In hoc uolumine continentur hec:
Historia Anglorum
Omelia super Cum loqueretur Ihesus ad turbas
Sermo de Trinitate
Sermo de Sancto Albano

The titles 'homily' and 'sermon' need not indicate that these texts were ever preached to William's congregation, however, for there were several different ways in which a twelfth-century monastic author could understand such terms.

If they were intended to be read aloud, or if they found their origin in William's preaching to the community, these sermons would most likely have been delivered to the Newburgh canons during their daily chapter. After Mass, monks or canons regular assembled to discuss their community's business, to mete out punishments, and to hear a sermon, usually delivered by the abbot or prior.[25] The length alone of William's texts, however, makes it unlikely that the canon had composed them with Newburgh Priory's chapter in mind. In his discussion of whether or not Bernard of Clairvaux's sermons on the Canticle of Canticles were ever preached, Jean Leclercq suggested that a sermon delivered in chapter would not have lasted for more than an hour (though some preachers, such as Bernard, could be granted exceptions).[26] That all three of these texts are at least twice the length that Leclercq determined was typical for a sermon indicates that they were not read in chapter.

25 This was the setting in which Gorman believed these sermons to have been delivered. Gorman, p. 19.

26 Leclercq, 'Were the Sermons on the Song of Songs Delivered in Chapter?' in Bernard of Clairvaux, *On the Song of Songs II*, trans. K. Walsh (Kalamazoo, Mich. 1976), pp. vii–xxx. Mark Zier supports the limit proposed by Leclercq for sermons composed by canons. Zier, 'Sermons of the Twelfth-Century Schoolmasters and Canons,' in Kienzle, *The Sermon*, p. 335.

While these three sermons nevertheless may have had their origin in William's preaching, in their present form they are wholly literary productions, with the terms 'omelia' and 'sermo' indicating that they were intended for private, meditative reading.[27] The following analyses of the individual sermons will demonstrate the ways in which William moves deftly between biblical allusions, juxtaposing passages otherwise unassociated by the patristic commentary tradition, as he received it. Further, William structures his sermons carefully, creating distinct sections, each with its own theological or exegetical argument; as William's medieval readers meditated upon his texts, they could relate these sections to one another in complex and subtle ways. The style of these sermons, therefore, appears symptomatic of texts intended to facilitate the monastic meditational practices described by Leclerçq and, more recently, Mary Carruthers.[28] William was very familiar with this sort of meditation: he prefaces his Canticle-commentary by noting that such rumination is necessary if one wishes to discover a coherent narrative in the Canticle.[29] Having followed such practices to form his own reading of the Canticle, in his sermons William produced texts intended for the same sort of monastic meditation.

Though it appears that they were not read aloud to the entire community, the sermons' focus on monastic life was intended to provide William's audience with material on which they

27 For this use of these terms, see Beverly Mayne Kienzle, 'Introduction,' in *The Sermon*, p. 159.

28 Leclercq, *The Love of Learning and the Desire for God: A Study of Monastic Culture*, trans. C. Misrahi, 3rd ed. (New York 1982); Mary Carruthers, *The Book of Memory: A Study of Memory in Medieval Culture* (Cambridge 1990); *eadem*, *The Craft of Thought: Meditation, Rhetoric, and the Making of Images* (Cambridge 1998). See also Rachel Fulton, 'Praying with Anselm at Admont: A Meditation on Practice,' *Speculum* 81 (2006) 700–733; Monika Otter, 'Entrances and Exits: Performing the Psalms in Goscelin's *Liber confortatorius*,' *Speculum* 83 (2008) 283–302.

29 *Explanatio* 1. Prol. (Gorman, p. 76). William accounts for the lack of chronological progression within the Canticle of Canticles by identifying it with these processes, the biblical author having jumbled the order the events and sayings of the *sponsa* and *sponsus*, William says, to facilitate the reader's meditation on the text. See also Fulton, *From Judgment to Passion*, pp 437–440.

could meditate, relating their monastic reading practices to the texts, doctrines, or figures discussed in his prose.

Sermo de Trinitate

William's sermon on the Trinity is not an abstract, theological reflection on the relationship between the three Persons of the Godhead, but rather a commentary on monastic liturgical practice. The canon offers an extended meditation on two of the major Trinitarian songs of the liturgy: the lesser doxology, 'Gloria Patri et Filio et Spiritui Sancto,' added to the end of verses from the Psalter whenever they are sung, and the 'Benedicamus Patrem et Filium cum Sancto Spiritu,' the versicle sung at first Vespers in the Office of the Trinity.[30]

Though it is not in any way divided in the manuscripts, this text does fall into several distinct sections. First, William discusses the history of these two verses, using references to the Trinity that he finds in various biblical texts to demonstrate that the *Gloria Patri* and *Benedicamus Patrem* derive from angelic song (lines 17–356). He then treats the verses' spiritual sense, showing that he and his audience of canons or monks also praise the Trinity with the 'mouth of their heart' and the 'throat of their mind,' i.e. with their pious thoughts and meditative devotion (lines 357–441), as well as through their *conversatio*, i.e. by living according to a monastic rule (lines 442–494). A person's ability to praise the Trinity, then, is itself Trinitarian: with song, with thought or meditation, and with action. William concludes his sermon by exploring this trinity of human praise (lines 495–555). The relationship between the modes of praise discussed in each of these sections is designed to be complex in a way that reflects the relationship between the Persons of the Trinity,

30 For the use of the *Gloria Patri* in the Office, see Frank Ll. Harrison, *Music in Medieval Britain* (Buren 1980), pp 58–61. On the *Benedicamus Patrem*, see CAO 2:454 (97a). For the use of the *Benedicamus* in the office of the Trinity in England, see Barbara C. Raw, 'The Office of the Trinity in the Crowland Psalter (Oxford, Bodleian Library, Douce 296),' *Anglo-Saxon England* 28 (1999) 193; the versicle can be seen in a manuscript reflecting English Benedictine use ca. 1200 in *Antiphonaire monastique: XIIe siècle, codex F. 160 de la Bibliothèque de la Cathédral de Worcester* (Tournay 1922), plate 162.

but William's treatment of the first topic, the angelic basis of Trinitarian song, which occupies the bulk of this sermon, is particularly elaborate; it therefore merits especial attention here.

Medieval liturgical commentaries frequently expressed the belief that the monastic liturgy, especially in its music, was related to the angels' worship of God in heaven. Liturgical song was seen as a medium through which the heavens and the earth might be united.[31] The writing of an anonymous tenth-century commentator on the Alleluia, the verse sung in the Mass immediately before the Gospel, captures this idea of a relationship between the heavenly and earthly choirs:

> Deinde cantatur 'Alleluia,' quod ex Hebraeo in Latinum interpretatum sonat, 'Laudate Deum'; nam 'Allelu,' dicitur, 'laudate'; 'Ia,' nomen Dei est, unum ex decem nominibus quibus vocatur Deus apud Hebraeos. 'Alleluia' autem primum in Novo Testamento additum est, dicente Joanne, 'Audivi vocem in coelo dicentium: Alleluia,' [Apoc 19:6], et quia hac voce angelos in coelo Deum laudare cognovimus, hujusmodi voce laudationis creditum est Deum delectari. Hoc quoque ideo canimus, ut eumdem Deum nos colere in terra ostendamus, qui etiam colitur ab angelis in coelo, et hoc ante lectionem evangelicam a cantore interponitur, ut laudetur ab omnibus, cujus gratia salvantur omnes.[32]

The two choirs are united in worshipping God, the commentator writes, and they use the same songs to do so. The earthly chorus can be confident that it is singing together with the angels, because it bases its songs on biblical attestations of angelic words: the earthly Church sings the Alleluia because John says that the angels sing the same.

In his first sermon, William uses the same strategies as this tenth-century commentator, arguing that the Church's Trinitarian verses, the *Gloria Patri* and the *Benedicamus*, are based on biblical reports of angelic song, and that the Church on earth therefore sings them in harmony with the heavens. As opposed to the Alleluia, though, which John specifically reports to be

31 For a discussion of this motif see Fassler, *Gothic Song*, pp 30–81; Lori Kruckenberg, 'Neumatizing the Sequence: Special Performances of Sequences in the Central Middle Ages,' *Journal of the American Musicological Society* 59 (2006) 243–317.

32 *De divinis officiis*, PL 101:1250, with some corrections.

said by angels, the words of the two Trinitarian verses are not to be found in the canon of Scripture. In his exposition of these liturgical songs, therefore, William has to rely on various biblical accounts of visionary experiences, in which the seer hears an angelic song that contains what William can interpret as a Trinitarian element.[33]

While comparing biblical visionary accounts, William distinguishes between their levels of authority in order to determine how best to read and reconcile their various descriptions of heaven. For William, as for the late antique and medieval tradition generally, the most authoritative visionary in the Bible was Paul, who describes the experience of a flight to heaven in 2 Cor 12:2–4. Paul's text gave rise to the belief, found throughout medieval visionary prose, that there were three heavens, and that Paul had reached the highest.[34]

The authority of Paul's vision was further established when medieval commentators, including William, read 2 Cor 12 in terms of a model of the different ways of seeing that Augustine first described in his *De Genesi ad litteram.*[35] Augustine distinguishes between three modes of sight: bodily sight, by which material bodies are perceived; spiritual sight, by which the images of bodies are perceived; and intellective sight, by which the forms of things themselves are perceived, free from any intermediary images or bodies. The medieval commentary tradition used this paradigm to interpret the reference to the *tertium coelum* in 2 Cor 12:2 as indicating that Paul's vision was purely intellective, and commentators in turn associated each of the three modes of sight with a different experience of heaven. For example, in the *Glossa ordinaria*, compiled formally ca. 1140, 2 Cor 12:2 is explained in terms of these modes of sight.

33 On the significance of the role music plays in medieval visionary writing, see Steven Rozenski, 'The Visual, the Textual, and the Auditory in Henry Suso's *Vita* or *Life of the Servant,*' *Mystics Quarterly* 34 (2008) 35–72.

34 For a comparable example by an Augustinian roughly contemporary to William, see Richard of St.-Victor, *De quattuor gradibus violentae caritatis*, in *Épître à Séverin sur la charité, les quatres degrés de la violente charité*, ed. G. Dumeige (Paris 1955), pp 126–177.

35 *De Genesi ad litteram* 12, ed. J. Zycha, CSEL 28:1 (Prague 1894), pp 379–435.

> *Vsque ad tertium celum.* Vel tres celi intelliguntur tria genera visionum, ut primum celum sit corporalis visio, cum corporaliter quedam videntur Dei munere, ut Helizeus vidit ignitos currus quando videlicet raptus est Helias [cf. 4 Reg 2:12], et Balthasar manum scribentem in pariete [cf. Dan 5:5]. ... Secundum celum est imaginaria vel spiritualis visio, quando aliquis in extasi vel somno videt non corpora, sed imagines rerum Dei reuelatione, ut Petrus discum [cf. Act 11:5]. Tertium celum est intellectualis visio, quando nec corpora nec imagines eorum videntur, sed in incorporeis substantiis intuitus mentis mira Dei potentia figitur. Ad hanc raptus est Apostolus, ut ipsum Deum in se, non in figura aliqua, videret.[36]

William believes in the authority of Paul's vision, therefore, because Paul saw in a purely intellective manner. William's other biblical sources, Isaiah, Ezechiel, and John, report seeing fantastic figures, which William, again following the commentary tradition, associates with spiritual sight and, therefore, the second heaven and a lesser degree of authority.

While William's account of the biblical sources of Trinitarian song must be based on Paul, his chief authority is unable to tell him anything about the content of the 'arcana uerba' which he heard. But perhaps, William suggests, Paul was hinting at the content of this heavenly song elsewhere in his writing, e.g. in Rom 11:36. Having proposed this possibility, William is then able to bring other visionary accounts to bear, even though they are less authoritative than Paul. Isaiah and John, though both seeing spiritually and therefore only reaching the second heaven, confirm William's suspicion about the relationship between 2 Cor 12:2 and Rom 11:36. Both the Old Testament prophet and the New Testament revelator agree on the Trinitarian quality of angelic song: in both accounts, the angels proclaim the threefold nature of God, 'Sanctus, Sanctus, Sanctus.'

36 *Biblia Latina cum Glossa Ordinaria: Facsimile reprint of the editio princeps, Adolph Rusch of Strassburg, 1480/81*, ed. M.T. Gibson and K. Froehlich (Turnhout 1992), vol. 4, p. 352. On the *Glossa*, see Gibson and Froehlich's introduction, as well as the introduction to Gilbertus Universalis, *Glossa Ordinaria in Lamentationes Ieremie Prophete*, ed. A. Andrée (Stockholm 2005), with bibliography.

Since they are spiritual, not intellective, these visions of the threefold 'Sanctus' of Isaiah and John are only an image of the truth of the Trinity, which Paul saw without mediation and was able to express in a more complete fashion, though still imperfectly, in Rom 11:36. All of these visions, therefore, reveal that the Trinitarian songs of the Church are sung in harmony with the Trinitarian songs of heaven. Further, on his way to this conclusion, we have seen that William relates the processes of seeing, hearing, and reading: just as he imagines monastic song to be a medium through which the heavens and the earth may be united, so too are scriptural allegory and mystical visions able, at least in part, to bridge the space between the truth above and the earth below.

Omelia super Cum loqueretur Ihesus ad turbas

William's devotion to the Virgin, developed at length in his Canticle-commentary, is illustrated in a more pithy form in the second of his shorter works.[37] This text is referred to as a 'homily' rather than a 'sermon' in the manuscripts (see the list of contents above), since William here concentrates on giving as complete an explanation as possible of his pericope, i.e. the biblical verse that he takes as his subject, Lc 11:27. The other two short works are both identified as 'sermons,' since, rather than focusing on a single verse, they are expositions of particular themes: the Trinity and St. Alban.[38] In this verse from Luke, which was read at the Vigil Mass of the Assumption,[39] a

37 William's Marian devotion is discussed at length in Fulton, *From Judgment to Passion*; *eadem*, 'Mimetic Devotion.' See also Gorman, pp 21–35.

38 See the distinction between a sermon and a homily presented in Kienzle, 'Introduction,' in *The Sermon*, pp 161–162.

39 A noted added to Lambeth, fol. 104r, identifies this text as the Gospel reading for the Vigil of the Assumption (see the notes on p. 61). This verse was associated with the Feast of Mary on August 15 in the earliest Roman usage: see Theodor Klauser, *Das Römische Capitulare Evangeliorum* (Münster 1935), pp 35, 81, 121, 161, and 180. Its English monastic use on the Vigil of the Assumption can be seen in the fourteenth-century Westminster Missal, *Missale ad Usum Ecclesie Westmonasteriensis*, ed. J.W. Legg (London 1891–1897), vol. 2, p. 909. A missal that survives from Lesnes Priory in Kent reflects English Augustinian use ca. 1200.

woman interrupts Jesus' preaching and shouts out in praise of his mother, 'Beatus uenter qui te portauit et ubera que suxisti.' As he interprets this exclamation, the structure William gives to his text allows him to demonstrate how this unnamed woman's few words confirm his beliefs about Mary, while also more generally exploring how he and his fellow canons ought best to approach the Gospels.

This homily is divided into two distinct sections: in the first, William presents his literal or historical interpretation of Luke's text, and, in the second, he offers a 'moral or mystical' reading of the same verse. Each section of the sermon begins with a decorated initial in the manuscripts, and each ends with its own doxology. William comments on this structure explicitly at the beginning of the second section (lines 345–348).

Presenting a literal interpretation of the woman's cry in Lc 11:27 could be problematic, however, since the evangelist provides no explanation of what she says, nor does he say anything about who she was or why she spoke as she did.[40] William therefore begins his exegesis by providing as full a contextualization as the biblical text allows: he describes Jesus casting a demon out of a man, the reaction of the pernicious Scribes and Pharisees to this miracle, and Jesus' response to them, in the middle of which the unnamed woman calls out in praise of Mary (lines 5–27). With the evangelist providing no further

---

Though it does not provide Gospel readings, this missal features the same proper collects, prayers, and verses for the Vigil of the Assumption as the Westminster Missal, and we may therefore conclude that Augustinians would also have used this Gospel reading at the Vigil Mass. *Missale de Lesnes*, ed. P. Jebb (Worcester 1964), pp 119 and 166. Lc 11:27 was also sung as an antiphon (CAO 1668) during Vespers and Matins in the octave of Christmas. For the history of Marian devotion in England, with particular reference to the history of various Marian feasts, see Mary Clayton, *The Cult of the Virgin Mary in Anglo-Saxon England* (Cambridge 1990). The changing trends in the liturgical celebration of the Virgin through the eleventh and twelfth centuries are discussed by Margot Fassler, 'Mary's Nativity, Fulbert of Chartres, and the *Stirps Jesse*: Liturgical Innovation ca. 1000 and Its Afterlife,' *Speculum* 75 (2006) 389–434.

40 Luke's vagueness gave medieval exegetes licence to interpret this verse quite creatively; see Alastair Minnis, *Translations of Authority in Medieval English Literature: Valuing the Vernacular* (Cambridge 2009) pp 215–216, n. 25.

explanation of this cry, it is up to William to account for the stages of cogitation that led the woman to call out as she did. Most of what remains in the first half of this homily is thus dedicated to William's description of how the woman was able to deduce from Jesus' speech that he was *perfectus Deus et perfectus homo*, and that his mother therefore was necessarily virginal and pure before and forever after his birth. This exegetical exploration, though perhaps an attempt to elucidate the literal sense of the passage, also exhibits a meditative quality, as William freely and creatively describes the woman's various thoughts and feelings, which resulted in her cry.

Tracing out the progress of the woman's thoughts provides William with a useful structuring device for the first half of this homily. At every stage of the woman's cogitation, William is able to bring various other biblical verses to bear, and his exegesis of these verses clarifies and nuances the woman's various realizations. Each stage also provides William with the opportunity to pause and explore the particular Marian doctrine that he believes to be relevant to what the woman had just thought. Much of his writing here is closely related to the description of Mary found in his Canticle-commentary: in the homily William presents the more succinct form of Marian themes developed at length in the commentary, and he sometimes borrows phrases or entire sentences from the longer work, relating them to the woman's exclamation in Lc 11:27.[41]

The second half of William's homily is just as carefully structured as the first. After acknowledging his poor ability to read 'morally or mystically,' William offers a simple moral interpretation of the expulsion of a demon that Jesus had undertaken before the woman's exclamation. He lists different types of *immundi spiritus* and the variety of vices with which they tempt men (lines 358–386). Likewise, he then reads the actions of the Scribes and Pharisees morally, comparing them

41 I have recorded several instances of this relationship in the notes, though I have by no means compared the two texts entirely. Further study should be undertaken regarding William's writing on Mary in these two sources. Though it seems likely that the Canticle-commentary antedates the sermon, this need not be the case: William could have been elaborating upon ideas presented in the sermon as he wrote the commentary.

to certain pernicious people in the Church of his own day; these scoffers, he says, believe that every pious act is inspired by hidden vanity (lines 387–401). Thus far William adheres clearly to his proclaimed intention of spiritual exegesis. When he reaches the point in the Lucan narrative at which the unnamed woman appears, however, William dramatically changes his expositional style. He first paraphrases Bede: 'Sane hanc mulierem siue ecclesie catholice siue pie cuiuslibet anime tipum gessisse dicamus, conueniens et ratum est,' (lines 416–418).[42] This statement appears to distract William from the task he has set for himself, for, immediately thereafter, he questions the purpose of allegorical reading altogether. Briefly discussing the theory behind his exegesis and its endorsement by the very authors of Scripture (cf. Gal 4:24–25), William concludes that reading allegorically is not meant to increase knowledge, but rather to sustain more ardent devotion to God (lines 438–444).[43]

No longer proceeding with a simple moral reading of the various events in Luke's account, as he had with the *immundi spiritus*, William creates an elaborate meditational structure for his discussion of the woman, and he develops this structure throughout the remainder of the second sermon. Having proclaimed that allegorical exegesis should support pious devotion, William then states that there are two ways to be devout: through fear or through joy. These modes correspond respectively to the *maiestas Dei* and the *dignatio Dei*. From here, though without acknowledging it until the very end of the sermon (lines 628–631), William uses the two elements of Lc 11:27, i.e. the *venter qui Christum portavit*, on the one hand, and, on the other, the *ubera quae Christus suxit*, as the basis for his exploration of several, ultimately interrelated dualities. Joy and fear, *maiestas* and *dignatio*, the Incarnation and the

42 William's statement may be compared to Bede, *In Lucam*, ed. D. Hurst, CCSL 120 (Turnhout 1960), p. 237: 'Et nos igitur his contra Eutichen dictis extollamus uocem cum ecclesia catholica cuius haec mulier typum gessit, extollamus et mentem de medio turbarum, dicamusque saluatori: Beatus uenter qui te portauit et ubera quae suxisti.'

43 For the problem of allegory in the Gospels and various medieval discussions concerning such exegesis, see Beryl Smalley, *The Gospels in the Schools, ca. 1100–ca.1280* (London 1985).

Church, Mary's fleshly and spiritual motherhood, and speech and devotion, amongst other pairs, are all discussed in turn, before William brings them together in the end of the sermon and identifies them as his spiritual reading of the woman's exclamation. In this way, William's structure provides his reader with a complex meditational exercise, charting the relationships that might exist between these various pairs.

Sermo de Sancto Albano

In the middle of the twelfth century, the relics of Alban, the British proto-martyr killed during the Diocletian persecutions ca. 304, were discovered and translated to the nearby Benedictine abbey bearing the saint's name. A member of that Hertfordshire community, William of St. Albans, soon recorded the event in his new *vita* of the saint, the *Alia acta Sancti Albani, Amphibali, et sociorum*, and the feast of Alban's *translatio*, August 2, was created.[44] The Benedictine William's account drew some material, especially the name Amphibalus for the priest that Alban housed, directly from Geoffrey of Monmouth's retelling of Alban's story, which Geoffrey (ca. 1100–ca. 1155) based on Gildas (d. ca. 570) rather than Bede.[45] William of Newburgh was one of Geoffrey's most acerbic critics, and he appears to have offered his own *Sermo de Sancto Albano* as a corrective to this new hagiographical tradition.[46] Basing his sermon on the authority of Bede's narrative, William was then

44 The *Alia acta Sancti Albani* is recorded in AASS, June 5 (1867), pp 129–138. For background on the cult of Alban, see Wilhelm Meyer, 'Die Legende des h. Albanus des Protomartyr Angliae in Texten vor Beda,' *Abhandlungen der Königlichen Gesellschaft der Wissenschaften zu Göttingen. Philologisch-Historische Klasse* n.f. 8 (1904) 3–81; see also the editor's introduction to John Lydgate, *The Life of Saint Alban and Saint Amphibal*, ed. J.E. van der Westhuizen (Leiden 1974), pp 26–44.

45 For the account of Alban in Geoffrey's work, see *Historia regum Britannie*, ed. N. Wright (Cambridge 1984), p. 48.

46 For William's criticism of Geoffrey, see the *Historia Anglorum* 1. Proem (Howlett, pp 11–19); see also David Rollo, 'Three Mediators and Three Venerable Books: Geoffrey of Monmouth, Mohammed, Chrétien de Troyes,' *Arthuriana* 8 (1998) 100–114.

free to explore various theological and exegetical matters surrounding the martyrdom, including Alban's nationality and his relationship to the English; the resulting text might best be considered 'variations on a theme by Bede.'

The *Sermo de Sancto Albano* is composed of a series of excursus based on the story of Alban's martyrdom found in Bede's *Historia* 1.7, which William identifies as his major source (line 126). Bede's version of the martyrdom is brief: Alban was a pagan Briton who sheltered a Christian prelate fleeing persecution; he admired the cleric's piety and was converted to Christianity, offering himself, disguised in the prelate's clothing, when pagan soldiers arrived at his door. Alban was interviewed by a pagan judge, refused to sacrifice to idols, and was executed. His death was accompanied by several miracles, all of which are included in William's *Sermo* (lines 513–559). William always returns faithfully to this 'theme' by Bede, in some instances borrowing or only slightly adapting Bede's diction.[47] In his 'variations,' William explores issues that arise from the various events of the story, e.g. whether martyrdom is a necessary or extraordinary thing (lines 409–494), or he offers exegesis of biblical verses that he believes to be relevant to Alban, e.g. Rom 10:17 and Act 1:1 apropos of the instruction Alban received from the cleric (lines 184 ff.).

While this structure affords William many opportunities to indulge in short digressions, two major 'variations' dominate his *Sermo*. The shorter of the two, already mentioned, occupies lines 409–494. Here, William argues that martyrdom is an extraordinary act and not a necessity, i.e. an act that God can require of any Christian, based on the definition of *necessaria* that he found in Hrabanus Maurus's Acts-commentary, apropos of Act 15:28.[48] In the other, longer digression (lines 16–125), William discusses Alban's conversion and martyrdom in terms of Cant 5:10 and 2:16, also making frequent reference to John's vision of the host of martyrs in Apoc 7:14. In tracing Alban's

47 See, for example, the notes on lines 227–229.

48 Hrabanus's Acts-commentary remains unedited; for a study of his other exegesis, see Matter, 'Exegesis and Christian Education,' pp 90–105, with bibliography.

progress from the blackness of his paganism, to the redness of his martyrdom, to his apocalyptic whiteness, William is able to compare Alban's death to Christ's crucifixion. As he recapitulates the theme at the end of the sermon (lines 560 ff.), William demonstrates that this relationship between Christ and Alban, i.e. that they can be discussed similarly in terms of these verses from the Canticle of Canticles, makes Alban a particularly exalted member of Christ's body.

The form of some of William's longer 'variations' is also notable, for William sometimes articulates his exegetical discussions as *quaestiones* (lines 220–311 and 409–494). After giving his initial interpretation of some element of Alban's story, William then raises an objection and offers a short argument to support a view contrary to the one he has just espoused. The problems with the alternative reading are then demonstrated, and William concludes with a stronger, refined version of his initial interpretation. Though this *quaestio* form was particularly favoured in scholastic writings, where it received its most elaborate treatment, we need not see William's use of this form as a sign of his participation in university culture. *Quaestiones* appear frequently in certain Carolingian biblical commentaries, on which we have already seen William drawing, and the influence of these Carolingian texts led to the use of *quaestiones* in other pre-scholastic or monastic commentaries of the twelfth century.[49] William spent almost all of his life in a priory in the North of England, and it therefore seems likely that his use of *quaestiones* was similarly inspired by Carolingian sources.

Finally, though it is shorter than the Acts- and Canticle-based 'variations,' the motif with which William both intro-

49 *Quaestiones* appear, for example, throughout the unedited Psalms-commentary of Remigius of Auxerre (d. 908). I have consulted this text in Rheims, Bibliothèque municipale, MS 132. On Remigius, see the essays collected in *L'École Carolingienne d'Auxerre*, ed. D. Iogna-Pratt et al. (Paris 1991); and Matter, 'Exegesis and Christian Education.' For an example of a pre-scholastic commentary that makes use of *quaestiones* deriving from its Carolingian source, see the discussion of the exegesis of Bruno le Chartreux by Jean Châtillon, 'La Bible dan les Écoles du XIIe siècle,' in *Le Moyen Age et la Bible*, ed. P. Riché and G. Lobrichon (Paris 1984), pp 163–197.

duces and concludes his sermon has implications that pervade his text. At both the beginning and the end of this sermon, William explores the question of Alban's nationality and how the saint relates to William's English audience (lines 2–15 and 621–649). In his development of this motif, William articulates more explicitly than anywhere in his *Historia* a definition of English identity after the Norman Conquest. The proper relationship between the British of Alban's time, which William associates with the twelfth-century Welsh, and William's fellow Englishmen is defined at the very beginning of the sermon as one of domination: though the Welsh or British must remain distinct from the English, the English have possession of them and control over them.[50] The idea of appropriation despite continued difference resurfaces at several different points in the sermon. For example, William uses the Canticle of Canticles colour motif, discussed above, to emphasize Alban's pagan origins, contrasting the blackness of his life with his final purity amid the crowd of martyrs. This colour symbolism is crucial, for even after Alban has become white, the wickedness of his pagan life is still noted: he is 'candidatus' rather than 'candidus' from birth.[51] The same motif also appears in William's account of Alban's entry into heaven (lines 560–572). Just as Alban has become a member united in heaven to his head, i.e. Christ, Alban's cult, though the saint is still British, has been incorporated into the greater body of the English Church. In William's sermon, the cultic devotion of the English to Alban is treated as a metonym for the relationship of the British to the English generally. Further, since William defines the English, his audience, exclusively in terms of their control of the British or Welsh, represented by Alban, he effaces the results of the Conquest, erasing any

50 William describes English domination of the British as necessitated by the latter's perfidy, a theme which he had already developed in the proem to Book One of his *Historia* (Howlett, p. 11).

51 The focus on a saint who is glorified in spite of his paganism is reminiscent of the Holy Innocents, and many of the verses William draws from the Apocalypse of John are shared with that feast. See Susan Boynton, 'Performative Exegesis in the Fleury *Interfectio Puerorum*,' *Viator* 29 (1998) 39–45.

distinction that might be drawn between the English and the Normans.

Certain themes emerge, therefore, that impart a sense of coherence to the exegetical portion of William's œuvre, i.e. to his Canticle-commentary and these three sermons. William uses the same language to describe Alban in his sermon and Mary in both his commentary and homily, often thinking of these two figures in terms of the same verses from the Canticle of Canticles. The shared priorities of his sermons on Lc 11:27 and on the Trinity are demonstrated by the similar exegesis of Apoc 3:15–16 that appears in each (lines 608–621 and 381–382, respectively), and by the common moral conclusion William reaches in both texts, concerning the spiritual meaning of the woman's exclamation (lines 589–621), on the one hand, and, on the other, the significance of the Trinitarian quality he finds in monastic life (lines 546–555). Further, while his use of the Canticle with regard to Alban relates that sermon to William's other exegetical writings, his use of Bede's *Historia* in the sermon and his discussion of English national identity necessarily bring his exegetical texts into conversation with his historical writings as well. The patterns that may be found in these three sermons bespeak the unity of William's writings more generally, suggesting that his *Historia* is best understood in light of the thematic concerns and hermeneutic practices found in his exegetical works.

Oxford, Bodleian Library, MS Rawlinson C. 31 (R)

Rawlinson is a small manuscript, measuring 210 mm by 140 mm and containing thirty-three parchment folios.[52] The first two gatherings, fols 1–13, contain William's *Sermo de Trini-*

52 Rawlinson is described by William D. Macray, *Catalogi Codicum Manuscriptorum Bibliothecae Bodleianae* (Oxford 1878), vol. 5.2, p. 9; Thomson, *Manuscripts from St. Albans Abbey*, vol. 1, p. 109; R.W. Hunt, 'The Library of St. Albans Abbey,' in *Medieval Scribes, Manuscripts, and Libraries: Essays Presented to N.R. Ker*, ed. M.B. Parkes and A.G. Watson (London 1978), pp 251–277, at 265. My thanks to Richard Rouse, who graciously reviewed parts of the following description.

tate (gathering 1; fols 1r–6v) and *Omelia super Cum loqueretur Ihesus ad turbas* (gathering 2; fols 7r–13v). The first gathering is written in single columns of thirty-two lines; the second has single columns of thirty-one lines. In the final two gatherings, fols 14r–31r contain glosses on Peter Comestor's *Historia scholastica*, from Gen 1 to Ex 28, written in a different hand in single columns of forty lines (incipit: 'Operi suo premittit magister prologum et prefacionem').[53] Fols 31v–33v are blank. Large rubricated initials begin new sections of the manuscript, and in William's sermons such initials appear on fols 1r and 7r; a rubricated 'H' is missing to begin the second section of the homily on Luke, though space was left for it by the scribe.

William's sermons in Rawlinson are written in an English book hand of the late twelfth century, influenced in its flourishes by contemporary English charter scripts. Slight changes in the *ductus* and habits of abbreviation over the course of the two texts suggest the possibility of the work being divided between two well-disciplined scribes.

The upper margin of fol. 1r in Rawlinson bears an inscription written in a mid-thirteenth-century hand: 'Hunc librum dedit dominus Fabianus supprior beato Albano. Quem qui ei abstulerit uel ab eius ecclesia alienauerit anathema sit.' This book curse indicates that the manuscript was given to the Benedictine Abbey of St. Albans in Hertfordshire by Fabian, who served as subprior there from ca. 1214 until his death in 1223. However, the hands of Rawlinson's scribes do not correspond to those of others active at St. Albans in this period, and it seems likely, therefore, that Fabian obtained the manuscript from outside the abbey.[54] The script, as well as a *terminus a quo* of after 1175 provided by the gloss on the *Historia Scholastica*, indicate that Rawlinson could not have been created too long before Fabian's subpriorship, and we may therefore date the manuscript to ca. 1200.

Rawlinson does not include William's sermon on St. Alban, and so it seems likely that its exemplar antedated that of the

53 See *Petri Comestoris Scholastica Historia, Liber Genesis*, ed. A. Sylwan, CCCM 191 (Turnhout 2005).

54 Thomson, *Manuscripts from St. Albans Abbey*, vol. 2, p. 63.

other manuscripts, which do contain the third text. Owing to its apparent earliness and the superiority of its text, Rawlinson has been used as the base manuscript for the two sermons which it contains. Rawlinson's text of William's sermons is particularly noteworthy: while in the other manuscripts William's sermons are appended to his *Historia Anglorum*, the existence of Rawlinson indicates that the sermons also circulated independently at the end of the twelfth century. Though Rawlinson's exemplar is lost and other manuscripts related to it are not forthcoming, Rawlinson suggests that William's homiletic writings could have had a wider readership than we might otherwise imagine, similar to that of his Canticle-commentary.

Rawlinson appears to have been in the possession of St. Albans until the Dissolution. There are no markings in the manuscript to indicate its ownership prior to Richard Rawlinson (1690–1755), whose manuscripts were given to the Bodleian upon his death.

London, British Library, MS Stowe 62 (S)

Stowe measures 270 mm by 177 mm and contains only works by William of Newburgh: the *Historia Anglorum* on fols 3r–158r and the three sermons on fols 159r–172r.[55] The text is written in double columns of thirty-two lines. The order of William's sermons in Stowe and Lambeth differs from that of Rawlinson, with the *Sermo de Trinitate* coming after the homily on Lc 11:27. A quire is missing between fols 166v and 167r in Stowe, resulting in the loss of the text of the *Sermo de Trinitate* after line 24 (i.e. only one column of the sermon's text is preserved) and of the *Sermo de Sancto Albano* before line 173 (see the notes on the relevant lines).

In his introduction to the *Historia*, Howlett described Stowe as 'a beautifully written copy in a hand of the twelfth century.'[56] Indeed, the pregothic hand of the manuscript's single scribe displays many tendencies which would suggest that the text

55 Stowe is described by Howlett, pp xl–xli; Hearne, vol. 1, pp x–xi; *Catalogue of the Stowe Manuscripts in the British Museum* (London 1895–1896), vol. 1, p. 40.

56 Howlett, p. xl.

was a product of the twelfth century.[57] Yet the events recorded in the *Historia*, as discussed above, provide a clear *terminus a quo* of mid-1198. It is most likely, then, that Stowe was produced early in the thirteenth century by a scribe with a conservative hand.[58]

Knowing where Stowe was made allows for a slightly greater degree of specificity with regard to its dating. Written in the same hand as the *Historia* and sermons, a table of contents on fol. 2v, quoted in full above (p. 8), identifies Stowe as a 'Liber Sancte Marie de Nouoburgo.' This identification of the book's ownership by the canons of Newburgh is confirmed by a note in a fourteenth-century hand in the upper margin of fol. 3r, reading 'Liber S. Mariae de Novo Burgo.' While we may therefore be certain that this manuscript was produced in William's priory, we cannot conclude, as other editors have,[59] that it was made in William's lifetime or very soon after his death. There are no known dated examples from Newburgh to which this text might be compared, and there is likewise no way of establishing that the scribal practices apparent in this manuscript did not continue at that priory several decades into the thirteenth century.[60] The only other manuscript known to

57 Hearne and the cataloguer of the Stowe collection state that the *Historia* is written in one hand, while the sermons and the table of contents on fol. 2v are written in a second, 'later hand of the thirteenth century.' *Catalogue of the Stowe Manuscripts*, vol. 1, p. 40; Hearne, vol. 1, pp x–xi. Yet I have been unable to find any changes in the scribe's *ductus* or in his habits of punctuation, spelling, or abbreviation between the *Historia* and the sermons. Further, the decorated initials in red, blue, and green that appear at the beginnings of the sermons (fols 159r, 163r, and 166v) are identical in form to their analogues in the body of the *Historia*, suggesting that the creation of the entire codex was undertaken as a single project. If Stowe was the work of more than one scribe, those scribes were contemporaries and engaged in their work at the same time.

58 In reconciling the twelfth-century tendencies of the scribe with the necessary date of the text, Howlett and the cataloguer of the Stowe collection concluded that this manuscript was produced ca. 1200. Howlett, pp xl–xli; *Catalogue of the Stowe Manuscripts*, vol. 1, p. 40.

59 Howlett, p. xxxix. Howlett cites the relationship between variants and corrections made on the various manuscripts of the *Historia* in favour of his conclusion. Howlett, p. xxxix, n. 1.

60 Ker, *Medieval Libraries of Great Britain*, p. 133.

bear a Newburgh *ex libris* from the period, British Library, MS Arundel 252, is clearly later than Stowe, dateable roughly to the second quarter of the century.[61] Treating Arundel as a *terminus ante quem*, it is most likely that Stowe was produced sometime in the first quarter of the thirteenth century.

Though Stowe was therefore produced at William's own priory, the inferiority of its text compared to Rawlinson disallows its use as the base manuscript for the homily on Lc 11:27. Likewise, its missing quire prevents it from being used as the base manuscript for the *Sermo de Sancto Albano*. It has only been used in the present edition to supply the sermons with titles and to give readings where Rawlinson and Lambeth appear incorrect.

The note on fol. 3r demonstrates that Stowe was still in the possession of Newburgh Priory in the fourteenth century. John Wells owned it in the sixteenth century (note on fol. 2r), and Sir Henry Spelman sold the manuscript on August 16, 1633 (note on fol. 2v). It was then bought by Sir Roger Twysden (note on the inside cover). When Hearne made his edition in 1719, the manuscript was owned by Sir Thomas Sebright. It then became part of the Stowe collection, was held by the Lords Ashburnham, and did not become available for study again until 1883, at which time Howlett used it for his edition.[62]

London, Lambeth Palace Library, MS 73 (L)

The manuscript of the works of William of Newburgh which now belongs to Lambeth Palace Library measures 335 mm by 237 mm. Written in double columns of forty-one lines in a hand of the early thirteenth century, it presents an early example of Gothic *littera textualis libraria*.[63] Two flyleaves have been added to both the beginning and the end of the codex, the former containing French homilies on the Gospels, and the latter a

61 For the relationship between these two manuscripts and others produced in Yorkshire in this period, see Lawrence-Mathers, 'A Northern English School?' pp 145–153, at 150–151; *eadem*, *Manuscripts in Northumbria*, pp 187–188.

62 Howlett, p. xli.

63 Lambeth is described by Jennifer Sheppard, *The Buildwas Books*, pp 114–119; James and Jenkins, *A Descriptive Catalogue*, pp 117–120.

fragment of a Psalter, glossed in French. William's *Historia Anglorum* occupies fols 1r–103r, and his three sermons are copied on fols 104r–121r. The final 30 folios contain the Latin text of the *Pastor Hermae*.[64]

William's texts in Lambeth appear to have been copied directly from Stowe or from a now-lost manuscript directly dependent upon Stowe. While there are many small errors and some longer clauses omitted from the body text in Lambeth, a smaller, contemporary glossing hand has offered marginal corrections and supplied all of the missing passages.[65] These marginalia bring Lambeth to a point of high coincidence with the text of Stowe. Because it contains the complete text of all three sermons, while Stowe is missing a quire, Lambeth has been used as the base manuscript for the sermon not found in Rawlinson. It has also been used to supply readings where Rawlinson's text of the first two sermons appears incorrect.

A note added in the final column of the *Historia* helps to determine the early ownership of the manuscript: it was produced for the English Cistercian house of Buildwas in Shropshire.[66] On fol. 103r, after the conclusion of William's *Historia*, and immediately before the beginning of his sermons, a later scribe has added:

> [A]nno Domini Millesimo Trecentesimo Primo. Contentione mota in capitulo generali apud Cistercium inter Abbates de Sauigniaco et de Bildewas, de paternitate domus Sancte Marie iuxta Dubiliniam, idem capitulum cognita ueritate tandem diffiniuit sic. Filiacionem Abbatie beate Marie iuxta Dubiliniam auditis rationibus utriusque partis et diligentius examinatis Abbati de Bildeuuas adiudicat capitulum generale.[67]

64 On the medieval interpretation of this second-century visionary text, see Theodore Bogdanos, 'The *Shepherd of Hermas* and the Development of Medieval Visionary Allegory,' *Viator* 8 (1977) 33–46.

65 Since this correcting hand is contemporary with the production of the body text, it has been favoured as the primary reading of the manuscript, and these marginalia are not indicated in the notes.

66 Though Sheppard, following James, notes the possibility that Lambeth was copied at Newburgh, she favours Buildwas as its place of origin. Sheppard, *Buildwas Books*, p. 118.

67 For the relationship between Buildwas and St. Mary's Abbey, Dublin, see Aubrey Gwynn and R. Neville Hadcock, *Medieval Religious Houses: Ireland* (London 1970), pp 130–131. See also Gwynn, 'The Origins of St.

Though it is only suggested in this note, the details of the scribe's hand and the decoration of the manuscript appear to confirm that Lambeth was created at Buildwas Abbey. The designs and colours used in its decorated initials correspond to a Cistercian style of the thirteenth century,[68] and, more specifically, its sharp, angular letter forms, the scribe's choice of abbreviations, the use of 'ci' for soft 'ti', and especially the use and peculiar form of the letter 'w' correspond to the characteristics of other Buildwas manuscripts from the second quarter of the thirteenth century, e.g. British Library, MS Harley 3038.[69] Therefore, while Lambeth must be later than Stowe, it could not have been created very long after its exemplar. We may date it roughly to the second quarter of the thirteenth century.

Little evidence survives to shed light on the provenance of this manuscript. The addition to the *Historia* quoted above indicates that it was still in the possession of Buildwas in the early fourteenth century. The Lambeth cataloguers suggest that a Greek inscription at the end of the manuscript could be that of Robert Talbot, a canon of Norwich in the mid sixteenth century.[70] The manuscript was brought into the collection at Lambeth Palace by Archbishop William Sancroft (d. 1690).[71]

Principles of the Edition

My goal in the creation of the present edition has been to provide the reader with the best possible text of William's sermons, while also preserving the orthography of the manuscripts from which that text is copied. The first two sermons are therefore transcribed from

---

Mary's Abbey, Dublin,' *Journal of the Royal Society of Antiquaries of Ireland* 79 (1949) 110–125.

68 See especially C.R. Cheney, 'English Cistercian Libraries: The First Century,' chapter in *Medieval Texts and Studies* (Oxford 1973), 328–345. See also Lawrence-Mathers, 'Northern English School?'; *eadem*, *Manuscripts in Northumbria*, 194–216.

69 For other comparable manuscripts, see Ker, *Medieval Libraries*, pp 14–15; Andrew G. Watson, *Medieval Libraries of Great Britain: A List of Surviving Books. Supplement to the Second Edition* (London 1987), p. 5. Jennifer Sheppard has argued for the existence of a sizeable scriptorium at Buildwas. 'The Twelfth-Century Library and Scriptorium at Buildwas: Assessing the Evidence,' in *England in the Twelfth Century: Proceedings of the 1988 Harlaxton Symposium*, ed. D. Williams (Woodbridge, Suffolk 1990), pp 193–204.

70 James and Jenkins, *A Descriptive Catalogue*, p. 120.

71 Sheppard, *Buildwas Books*, 119.

Rawlinson, and the final sermon is transcribed from Lambeth. With regard to the first two sermons, apparent errors in Rawlinson's text have been corrected with readings supplied from Lambeth or Stowe; in the final sermon, such readings have been supplied from Stowe. In the very few cases where all of the manuscripts appear to contain an error, I have provided my own corrected reading. All changes to the reading found in the base manuscript are recorded in the notes.

I have imposed modern punctuation and a paragraph structure on the text. For the sake of clarity and ease of reading, proper nouns, including the *nomina sacra*, have been capitalized throughout the sermons; common nouns or substantive adjectives that refer to God (e.g. *Veritas*, *Altissimus*, etc.) are similarly capitalized. The homily on Lc 11:27 is divided into two parts in the manuscripts, each beginning with a decorated initial and ending with a doxology, prefaced in Stowe and Lambeth by the pericope ('Cum loqueretur ...') with its own decorated initial. To translate the sense of this structure to a modern printed edition, I have divided the text into two sections, with one Roman numeral after the pericope and a second between the two halves of the homily.

The notes record the direct quotations and the allusions William makes to his biblical, patristic, and medieval sources. Quotations which William reproduces without any alteration, apart from his frequent omission of a postpositive conjunction (e.g. *etiam* or *autem*) or other slight modifications, are noted simply. When it appears that William has intentionally modified his source to fit it into his prose or has remembered some of it incorrectly, the corresponding note begins 'cf.' The abbreviations of biblical books and the enumeration of the Psalms follow the Colunga-Turrado edition of the Vulgate, while the English names of biblical books are taken from the Douay translation.

When William indicates that he is quoting from a biblical source, the quotation is given in italic print. Similarly, a text that is the subject of William's exegesis, even if it is not biblical, appears in italic print: this principle pertains especially to the *Sermo de Trinitate*, where William presents his interpretation of extra-biblical, liturgical texts. Other non-biblical and patristic quotations appear in quotation marks. Biblical references made in passing, i.e. those that William does not signal as being quotations, are not distinguished from the rest of the text of the sermon, though they are recorded in the notes. William's biblical quotations and allusions are collated in an index that follows the text of the sermons.

SELECT BIBLIOGRAPHY

Primary Sources

Bede. *Historia ecclesiastica gentis Anglorum*. Ed. and trans. B. Colgrave and R.A.B. Mynors (Oxford 1969).

William of Newburgh. *Guilielmi Neubrigensis Historia sive Chronica rerum anglicarum*. 3 vols. Ed. Thomas Hearne (Oxford 1719).

———. *Historia rerum Anglicarum*. In *Chronicles of the Reigns of Stephen, Henry II, and Richard I*. Vol. 1, p. i–vol. 2, p. 583. Ed. R. Howlett (London 1884–1885).

———. *William of Newburgh's Explanatio sacri epithalamii in matrem sponsi: A Commentary on the Canticle of Canticles (12th-C.)*. Ed. J.C. Gorman (Fribourg 1960).

———. *The History of English Affairs: Book I*. Trans. P.G. Walsh and M.J. Kennedy (Warminster 1988).

———. *The History of English Affairs: Book II*. Trans. P.G. Walsh and †M.J. Kennedy (Oxford 2007).

Secondary Studies

Biller, Peter. 'William of Newburgh and the Cathar Mission to England.' In *Life and Thought in the Northern Church, c. 1100–c. 1700. Essays in Honour of Claire Cross*, ed. D. Wood (Woodbridge, Suffolk 1999). Pp 11–30.

Brooke, C.N.L. Review of *Explanatio*, ed. Gorman. *English Historical Review* 77 (1962) 554.

Burton, Janet. *The Monastic Order in Yorkshire, 1069–1215* (Cambridge 1999).

———. 'The Settlement of Disputes between Byland Abbey and Newburgh Priory.' *Yorkshire Archaeological Journal* 55 (1983) 67–72.

Clay, Charles Travis. 'The Early Abbots of Yorkshire Cistercian Houses.' *Yorkshire Archaeological Journal* 38 (1955) 8–43.

———. *Early Yorkshire Charters*. 10 vols (Wakefield 1935–1965).

Cohen, Jeffrey Jerome. *Hybridity, Identity, and Monstrosity in Medieval Britain: On Difficult Middles* (New York 2006).

Cooper, Janet M. *The Last Four Anglo-Saxon Archbishops of York* (York 1970).

Dahan, Gilbert. *L'exégèse chrétienne de la Bible en Occident médiéval, XIIe-XIVe siècle* (Paris 1999).

Dickinson, John C. *The Origins of the Austin Canons and their Introduction into England* (London 1950).

Fassler, Margot E. 'The Office of the Cantor in Early Western Monastic Rules and Customaries: A Preliminary Investigation.' *Early Music History* 5 (1985) 29–51.

———. *Gothic Song: Victorine Sequences and Augustinian Reform in Twelfth-Century Paris* (Cambridge 1993).

Fulton, Rachel. *From Judgment to Passion: Devotion to Christ and the Virgin Mary, 800–1200* (New York 2002).

———. 'Mimetic Devotion, Marian Exegesis, and the Historical Sense of the Song of Songs.' *Viator* 27 (1996) 85–116.

Gillingham, John. 'The Historian as Judge: William of Newburgh and Hubert Walter.' *English Historical Review* 119 (2004) 1275–1287.

———. 'Royal Newsletters, Forgeries, and English Historians.' In *La Cour Plantagenêt (1154–1204)*, ed. M. Aurell (Poitiers 2000). Pp 171–185.

———. 'Two Yorkshire Historians Compared: Roger of Howden and William of Newburgh.' *The Haskins Society Journal* 12 (2002) 15–37.

———. 'William of Newburgh and Emperor Henry VI.' In *Auxilia Historica. Festschrift für Peter Acht*, ed. W. Koch et al. (Munich 2001). Pp 51–71.

Gransden, Antonia. 'Bede's Reputation as an Historian in Medieval England.' Chapter in *Legends, Traditions, and History in Medieval England* (London 1992). Pp 1–29.

———. *Historical Writing in England, ca. 550 to ca. 1307*. 2 vols (Ithaca 1974).

Herbert, Jane. 'The Transformation of Hermitages into Augustinian Priories in Twelfth-Century England.' *Studies in Church History* 22 (1985) 131–145.

Hesbert, René-Jean. *Corpus Antiphonalium Officii*. 6 vols (Rome 1963–1979).

Jahncke, Rudolf. *Guilelmus Neubrigensis. Ein pragmatischer Geschichtsschreiber des zwölften Jahrhunderts* (Bonn 1912).

James, Montague Rhodes, and Claude Jenkins. *A Descriptive Catalogue of the Manuscripts in the Library of Lambeth Palace* (Cambridge 1930–1932).

Kennedy, M.J. '"Faith in the one God flowed over you from the Jews, the sons of the patriarchs and the prophets": William of Newburgh's Writings on Anti-Jewish Violence.' *Anglo-Norman Studies* 25 (2002) 139–152.

Ker, N.R. *Medieval Libraries of Great Britain: A List of Surviving Books*. 2nd ed. (London 1964).

Kienzle, Beverly Mayne, ed. *The Sermon*. Typologie des sources du Moyen Age occidental 81–83 (Turnhout 2000).

Lawrence-Mathers, Anne E. *Manuscripts in Northumbria in the Eleventh and Twelfth Centuries* (Woodbridge, Suffolk 2003).

———. 'A Northern English School? Patterns of Production and Collection of Manuscripts in Augustinian Houses of Yorkshire in the Twelfth and Thirteenth Centuries.' In *Yorkshire Monasticism: Archaeology, Art, and Architecture from the 7th to the 16th Centuries*, ed. L. R. Hoey (Leeds 1995). Pp 145–153.

———. 'William of Newburgh and the Northumbrian Construction of English History.' *Journal of Medieval History* 33 (2007) 339–357.

Matter, E. Ann. 'Exegesis and Christian Education: The Carolingian Model.' In *Schools of Thought in the Christian Tradition*, ed. P. Henry (Philadelphia 1984). Pp 90–105.

Otter, Monika. '1066: The Moment of Transition in Two Narratives of the Norman Conquest.' *Speculum* 74 (1999) 565–586.

———. *Inventiones: Fiction and Referentiality in Twelfth-Century English Historical Writing* (Chapel Hill 1996).

Partner, Nancy. *Serious Entertainments: The Writing of History in Twelfth-Century England* (Chicago 1977).

Rollo, David. *Historical Fabrication, Ethnic Fable, and French Romance in Twelfth-Century England* (Lexington 1998).

———. 'Three Mediators and Three Venerable Books: Geoffrey of Monmouth, Mohammed, Chrétien de Troyes.' *Arthuriana* 8 (1998) 100–114.

Sheppard, Jennifer. *The Buildwas Books: Book Production, Acquisition, and Use at an English Cistercian Monastery, 1165–c. 1400* (Oxford 1997).

Stegmüller, Friedrich. *Repertorium Biblicum Medii Aevi*. 7 vols (Madrid 1950–1961); completed by Nicholaus Reinhardt. 4 vols (Madrid 1978–1980).

Thompson, A. Hamilton. *History and Architectural Description of the Priory of St. Mary, Bolton-in-Wharfedale, with some account of the Canons Regular of the Order of St. Augustine and their Houses in Yorkshire* (Leeds 1928).

Thomson, Rodney M. *Manuscripts from St. Albans Abbey, 1066–1235*. 2 vols (Woodbridge, Suffolk 1982).

Wormald, Francis. 'A Liturgical Calendar from Guisborough Priory, with Some Obits.' *Yorkshire Archaeological Journal* 31 (1934) 5–35.

I Sermo de Trinitate

Edited from

Oxford, Bodleian Library, MS Rawlinson C. 31, fols 1r-6v

SERMO DE TRINITATE

Benedicamus Patrem et Filium cum Sancto Spiritu. Hoc sol- *1r*
lempniter, hoc frequenter, hoc suauiter cantat ecclesia. Sed numquid ecclesia peregrinorum, et non magis ecclesia ciuium? Numquid hoc cantant homines, et non cantant angeli? Numquid hoc canitur in mari, et non canitur in portu; canitur in uia, et non canitur in patria? Immo multo sollempnius atque suauius ab angelis quam ab hominibus, in portu quam in mari, in patria quam in uia. Rauce hoc canunt homines, clare angeli. Quippe homines dum aquam turbidam de torrente in uia bibunt, uocis claritatem habere non possunt; porro angeli aquam limpidam de fonte uite hauriunt, et ideo clare canunt. Cum autem homines, iuxta promissionem dominicam, equales angelis fuerint, tunc nemo rauce cantabit, sed ab ore omnium *Benedicamus Patrem et Filium cum Sancto Spiritu* clare et dulciter reboabit.

Et quidem ab initio angeli hoc cecinere, ex quo scilicet diuisit Deus lucem a tenebris. Facta est lux, Deo dicente, 'Fiat lux.' Facte sunt et tenebre, sed non Deo dicente, 'Fiant tenebre.' Nempe auctor lucis est et non tenebrarum. Denique electi angeli, a sue creationis initio ad creatorem se conuertentes, facti sunt lux, alii uero auertentes se ab eo, facti sunt tenebre. Illi adherendo uere luci, facti sunt lux in Domino, hii uero uolentes esse lux in se et non in Domino, facti sunt ferales et dense tenebre. Verum non Deo auctore facti sunt tenebre, quia numquam dixit Deus, 'Fiant tenebre.' Itaque seipsis auctoribus facti sunt tenebre. Porro electi angeli non seipsis auctoribus facti sunt

2 *Benedicamus...Spiritu*: CAO 6238/7966. Subsequent quotations of this versicle will not be noted.
18 *diuisit...tenebris*: cf. Gen 1:4.
Facta...lux: cf. Gen 1:3.
20–22 *Denique...lux*: cf. Augustine, *De civitate Dei* 11.9 and 11.33 (CCSL 48, pp 329–330 and 352–354; PL 41:325 and 346–347).
24–25 *dense tenebre*: cf. Ex 10:21.

1 SERMO DE TRINITATE *supplied from a list of contents on fol. 2v S : omitted by R : omitted by L, which here reads* Item tractatus eiusdem ad eundem super hunc versum: Benedicamus Patrem et Filium cum Sancto Spiritu **2** Sancto Spiritu *LS* : Spiritu Sancto *R* **24–578** lux...Amen *here a quire is missing in S*

lux, sed ipso auctore qui ait, ‘Fiat lux.’ Et diuisit Deus lucem a tenebris, id est magnum chaos firmauit inter hos et illos, ut neque hii ad illos transire, neque illi ad hos ualeant transmeare; illis celum pro merito dignitatis attribuens, hos uero angelica nudatos gloria in aerem caliginosum detrudens, unde et aerii spiritus dicuntur. Hac igitur diuisione facta, hoc chao firmato inter hos et illos, uidentes electi angeli quod essent lux et scientes non solum in quo, sed etiam quo auctore essent lux, in gratiarum actione se totos dederunt, et pro sue beatificationis leticia sollempnes choros ducentes claris uocibus cantare ceperunt, *Benedicamus Patrem et Filium cum Sancto Spiritu.*

Inde est quod Ysaias cum se Dominum sedentem super solium excelsum uidisse dixisset, et circa illum seraphin, id est sublimes illos spiritus pro eo quod caritate conditoris ardeant tali uocabulo designatos, adiunxit, *Et clamabant alter ad alterum et dicebant, ‘Sanctus, Sanctus, Sanctus, Dominus Deus exercituum.’* In eo quod dicitur, *Sanctus, Sanctus, Sanctus*, personarum Trinitas, in eo uero quod additur, *Dominus Deus*, exprimitur substantie unitas. Sic igitur dicitur, *Sanctus, Sanctus, Sanctus, Dominus Deus*, ac si diceretur, ‘Pater et Filius et Spiritus Sanctus, unus Deus.’ Hoc clamant seraphin alter ad alterum, scilicet ad laudandam communibus tam uotis quam uocibus creatricem et beatificatricem Trinitatem inuicem se exhortantes et quasi sollempniter inuitantes. Nonne hoc est, *Benedicamus Patrem et Filium cum Sancto Spiritu*? Siquidem *Benedicamus* uox est alterius ad alterum inuitantis ad conbenedicendum. Porro quia hec uox in / angelis pro sue conuersionis et confirmationis *1v*

28 *Fiat lux*: Gen 1:3.
28–29 *Et…tenebris*: cf. Gen 1:4.
29–30 *magnum…transmeare*: Lc 16:26 (Vetus Latina).
39–40 *Dominum…excelsum*: Is 6:1.
40 *circa illum seraphin*: *seraphin* is a second object of *uidisse*, with *illum* referring to *Dominum*; cf. Is 6:1–2.
41–42 *sublimes…designatos*: cf. Isidore of Seville, *Etymologiarum siue originum* VII.v.24–25 (ed. Lindsay).
42–44 *Et…exercituum*: Is 6:3.
53 *ad conbenedicendum*: ‘to a communal act of blessing’; cf. line 49: *ad laudandum communibus tam uotis quam uocibus.*
54 *conuersionis*: cf. line 21 above.

33 chao : chaos *RL*

leticia clara et sollempnis est, non simpliciter uox sed clamor dicitur a propheta. Itaque angeli ab initio clamant, *Sanctus, Sanctus, Sanctus, Dominus Deus exercituum*, id est sollempniter concinunt, *Benedicamus Patrem et Filium cum Sancto Spiritu*. Sic inquam canit et sic ab initio cecinit chorus angelicus, numquam deinceps a laude cessaturus. Vnde in eodem cantico subditur, *Laudemus et superexaltemus eum in secula*. Denique hinc ad nos uenit hoc canticum, et pro modulo suo humana deuotio concentum imitatur angelicum, nichil habens in ore dulcius, nichil frequentius quam, *Gloria Patri et Filio et Spiritui Sancto*.

Raptus est Paulus usque ad tercium celum, interfuit choris angelicis, et Deum quidem ibi audiuit dicentem sibi archana uerba que non licet homini loqui. Porro angelos audiuit sollempniter canentes, atque inde huc rediens iuxta quod ibi didicerat et ipse cecinit et ecclesiam canere docuit. Audi stupentem et canentem: stupentem pro uerbis illis archanis que audierat, canentem uero iuxta quod angelos canentes audierat. *O altitudo*, inquit, *diuiciarum, sapientie, et scientie Dei, quam incomprehensibilia sunt iuditia eius et inuestigabiles uie eius*. Ecce, hec est uox stupentis pro uerbis illis archanis que non licet homini loqui. Sequitur: *Quoniam ex ipso et per ipsum et in ipso sunt omnia, ipsi gloria in secula. Amen*. Ecce, hec est uox canentis et formam canendi ecclesie tradentis, iuxta quod angelos canentes audierat, dicens, *Ex ipso et per ipsum et in ipso sunt omnia*, personarum Trinitatem, et adiungens, *Ipsi gloria*, substantie designauit unitatem. *Ipsi*, inquit, *gloria*. Cui? Ex quo, per quem, in quo omnia. Nonne hoc est quod ecclesia tam crebro canit, *Gloria Patri et Filio et Spiritui Sancto*?

56–57 *Sanctus…exercituum*: Is 6:3.
61 *Laudemus…secula*: CAO 6238/7966.
66 *Raptus…celum*: cf. 2 Cor 12:2.
67–68 *audiuit…loqui*: cf. 2 Cor 12:4.
73–74 *O…eius*: Rom 11:33.
75–76 *uerbis…loqui*: cf. 2 Cor 12:4.
76–77 *Quoniam…Amen*: Rom 11:36.
79–82 *Ex…gloria*: cf. Rom 11:36.

68–69 audiuit sollempniter *L* : sollempniter audiuit *R* **83** crebro *L* : crebo *R*

Quippe in his uerbis ecclesiasticis apostolicorum sensus uerborum integer est. Vt autem ecclesia, integre retento sensu apostolico, uerbis propriis caneret, propter simpliciores factum est qui apostolicorum profunditatem uerborum penetrare non poterant. Siquidem uerborum sublimium istorum, *Ex ipso, per ipsum, in ipso sunt omnia, ipsi gloria in secula, amen*, sancta simplicitas expressionem requirebat. Satisfecit ei ecclesia in Nicena Sinodo, et uerba illa ex puteo alto apostolici pectoris manancia ac per hoc supra modum simplicium ponderosa facilioribus et expressioribus uerbis mutauit, ut caneretur sic: *Gloria Patri et Filio et Spiritui Sancto in secula seculorum. Amen*. Nam quod interponitur, *Sicut erat in principio et nunc et semper*, beatus Ieronimus interposuisse dicitur. Itaque uerbis illis apostolicis et ecclesiasticis idem omnino dicitur uel canitur: illis quidem pro apostolica dignitate sublimius, istis uero expressius propter filias Ierusalem, id est animas simpliciores. Sic igitur per Apostolum raptum usque ad tercium celum atque inde ad nos redeuntem forma concentus angelici ad nos usque peruenit.

Quod autem Paulus a tercio celo, ubi scilicet non per imaginationes sed nuda et perspicua conspicitur ueritas, hoc pro-

85–89 *Quippe…poterant*: William asserts that the 'sense' of Rom 11:36 is preserved in the two liturgical canticles, the *Benedicamus* and the *Gloria Patri*. The Church uses these canticles out of necessity, he says, because the profundity of Rom 11:36 is too subtle for the simpler members of the Church to grasp.

91–97 *Satisfecit…dicitur*: cf. Ps-Jerome, *Epistola* 47.1 (PL 30:295). The attribution of this letter to Jerome is spurious, though it circulated under his name throughout the Middle Ages. In this letter, the Ps-Jerome states that the Council of Nicaea endorsed the use of the *Gloria Patri*. William believes that the Nicaean Council supported a simplified translation of the sense of Rom 11:36, and he therefore attributes the phrase, *Sicut erat in principio et nunc et semper*, to Jerome based on his observation that, while the Ps-Jerome advocated the use of the *Gloria Patri* in its complete form, the *Sicut erat* does not correspond to anything found in Rom 11:36. The object of *mutauit* (line 94) is *uerba illa manancia ac ponderosa* (lines 92 and 93).

100 *propter…Ierusalem*: Cant 3:10.

101 *raptum…celum*: 2 Cor 12:2.

104–107 *Quod…palliata*: cf. Augustine, *De Genesi ad litteram libri duodecim* 12, especially 12.6 (CSEL 28.1, pp 386–387; PL

culdubio Ysaias nobis detulit a medio celo, ubi scilicet ueritas non cernitur nuda et mera, sed misticis imaginibus palliata. Non enim Paulus aliquid corporeum uel quasi corporeum se refert / uidisse; Ysaias uero sic narrat: *Vidi Dominum sedentem* 2r *super solium excelsum, et ea que sub ipso erant implebant templum. Seraphin stabant super illud, sex ale uni et sex ale alteri. Duabus uelabant faciem eius, et duabus pedes eius, et duabus uolabant. Et clamabant alter ad alterum, 'Sanctus, Sanctus, Sanctus, Dominus Deus exercituum, plena est omnis terra gloria eius.'* Ecce, per quantas imaginum figuras menti prophetice ueritas refulgebat. Non ergo Ysaias ultra medium celum raptus erat. Ibi sane hoc ipsum audiuit angelos canentes quod Paulus in tercio celo, sed aliter, sicut et hoc ipsum ibi uidit quod Paulus in tercio celo, sed aliter. Quippe in tercio celo, ubi uere et non per enigmata ueritas auditur et cernitur, nec corpus nec quasi corpus cernitur, nec sonus nec quasi sonus auditur. Porro in medio celo non corpus sed quasi corpus cernitur, nec sonus sed quasi sonus auditur.

Denique uterque Dominum uidit, sed ille uere, hic specialiter; ille scilicet sicuti est, hic uero sedentem et uelatum alis

---

34:458–459). As is the case here, the medieval commentary tradition associated each of the three Augustinian 'modes of sight' with one of the three heavens. See, e.g., the *Glossa ordinaria* on 2 Cor 12:2, ed. M.T. Gibson and K. Froehlich (Turnhout, 1992), vol. 4, p. 352, quoted in the Introduction above, p. 13. Paul reached the third or highest heaven, where he saw the truth itself, free from any intermediary bodies or images of bodies; Isaiah reached only the second heaven, where he saw the truth mediated by the images of bodies; the first or lowest heaven, according to this schema, is the firmament in which birds fly and where most of what is seen consists of bodies.

109–115 *Vidi…eius*: Is 6:1–3.

115–123 *Ecce…auditur*: cf. Augustine, *De Genesi ad litteram libri duodecim* 12.6 (CSEL 28.1, pp 386–387; PL 34:1028–1029); see the note on lines 104–107. William has added a discussion of sound and 'quasi-sound' to what was traditionally a visual schema; these two ways of hearing correspond respectively to seeing bodies (i.e. in the first heaven) and seeing images of bodies (i.e. in the second heaven).

120 *per enigmata*: cf. 1 Cor 13:12.

124–125 *specialiter*: 'according to appearance,' i.e. in a specific or limited way.

seraphin. Vterque etiam angelos Deo laudem canentes audiuit, sed ille in tercio celo neque per sonum neque tanquam per sonum, hic uero in medio celo non per sonum sed tanquam per sonum. Vnde dicit, *Et clamabant alter ad alterum, 'Sanctus, Sanctus, Sanctus, Dominus Deus exercituum, plena est omnis terra gloria eius.'* Quod utique non est aliud quam illud quod Paulus nobis attulit a tercio celo, scilicet, *Ex ipso et per ipsum et in ipso sunt omnia, ipsi gloria in secula.* Ecclesia uero formam canendi—et a medio primum celo per Ysaiam et a tercio postmodum celo per Paulum—sibi allatam cum exultatione suscipiens, et sanctum ex quo omnia Patrem, sanctum per quem omnia Filium, sanctum in quo omnia Spiritum Sanctum catholica ratione intelligens, suis magis uerbis canendo utitur propter simplices uerborum apostolicorum et propheticorum minus capaces. Denique seraphin clamantes alter ad alterum, *Sanctus, Sanctus, Sanctus*, ita imitatur, *Benedicamus Patrem et Filium cum Sancto Spiritu.* Illud uero apostolicum, *Ex ipso et per ipsum et in ipso sunt omnia, ipsi gloria*, propriis uerbis ita canit, *Gloria Patri et Filio et Spiritui Sancto.*

Iohannes quoque usque ad medium celum raptus est, ibique audiuit canentia quatuor animalia et eisdem pene uerbis quibus Isaias ibidem seraphin clamantes audierat. Raptum se indicat cum dicit, *Statim fui in spiritu.* Et quousque raptus sit consequenter insinuat: *Et ecce*, inquit, *sedes posita erat in celo, et supra sedem sedens. Et qui sedebat similis erat aspectui lapidis iaspidis et sardini. Et iris erat in circuitu sedis similis uisioni smaragdine, et in circuitu sedis sedilia uiginti quatuor, et super thronos uiginti quatuor seniores sedentes circumamictos uestimentis albis. Et de throno procedunt fulgura et uoces et tonitrua; et septem lampades ardentes ante thronum, qui sunt septem spiritus Dei. Et in conspectu sedis tanquam mare uitreum simile cristallo. Et in medio sedis et in circuitu sedis quatuor animalia plena oculis ante et retro, et animal primum simile leoni, et secundum animal simile uitulo, et tercium*

139–140 *propter…capaces*: 'on account of the simple people less capable of comprehending the apostolic and prophetic words.'

148 *Statim…spiritu*: Apoc 4:2.

149-162 *Et…oculis*: Apoc 4:2–8.

animal habens / faciem quasi hominis, et quartum animal si- 2v
mile aquile uolanti. Et singula eorum habebant alas senas, et in circuitu et intus plena sunt oculis.

His uerbis satis ostendit quousque raptus fuerit, scilicet usque ad medium celum, ubi ueritas non perspicue et nude sed per figurarum enigmata quasi in speculo cernitur. Nam in tercio celo, quo raptus est Paulus, non imago aliqua sed ueritas ipsa conspicitur. Et sicut ibi Iohannes corpora non uidit sed similitudines corporum, ita etiam sonos non audiuit sed similitudines, ut ita dicam, sonorum. Vnde signanter in sequentibus dicit, *Et audiui uocem de celo tanquam uocem aquarum multarum et tanquam uocem tonitrui magni, et uocem quam audiui sicut cytharedorum citharizantium in cytharis suis*. Non dicit se audisse uocem aquarum multarum aut tonitrui magni aut cytharedorum, sed per *tanquam* et *sicut* indicat se non tales sonos aure corporali, sed talium similitudines sonorum aure hausisse spirituali. Hoc modo etiam quatuor animalium uocem audiuit, de quibus sic loquitur, *Et requiem non habebant die ac nocte, dicentia, 'Sanctus, Sanctus, Sanctus, Dominus Deus omnipotens, qui erat et qui est et qui uenturus est.'*

Requiem, inquit, *non habebant*. Est enim requies ab actione, est et requies a passione. Cum Dominus dicit, *Tollite iugum meum super uos et discite a me, quia mitis sum et humilis corde, et inuenietis requiem animabus uestris*, requies a molestia passionis intelligitur. At cum dicitur requieuisse Deus ab operibus suis, requies ab actione significatur. Quippe requieuit, id est cessauit, Deus a nouarum specierum conditione, qui non requiescit, id est non cessat, cotidie a conditarum specierum administratione. Vnde et Dominus dicit,

163–169 *His...sonorum*: cf. Augustine, *De Genesi ad litteram libri duodecim* 12.6 (CSEL 28.1, pp 386–387; PL 34:1028–1029).
164–5 *sed...cernitur*: cf. 1 Cor 13:12.
169 *signanter*: 'clearly, expressly.'
170–172 *Et...suis*: Apoc 14:2.
177–179 *Et...est*: Apoc 4:8.
180 *Requiem...habebant*: Apoc 4:8.
181–183 *Tollite...uestris*: Mt 11:29.
184–185 *requieuisse...suis*: cf. Gen 2:2, Hebr 4:10.

168 sonos non *L* : non sonos *R*

Pater meus usque modo operatur et ego operor. Hoc modo dicitur de quatuor animalibus quod requiem non habebant, id est cessationem a laude Dei. Est bona requies, est et mala requies. Requies bona est qua cessatur a malis; hanc habebant. Mala uero requies est qua cessatur a bonis; hanc non habebant que iugiter dicebant, *Sanctus, Sanctus, Sanctus, Dominus Deus omnipotens.*

Itaque non tantum Ysaias sub Veteri Testamento sed etiam Iohannes sub Nouo hanc canendi formam detulit nobis a medio celo, ubi non ueritas nuda sed imaginibus palliata conspicitur et auditur. Nempe primum, id est infimum, celum est, ut ascendendo computemus, ubi uidentur sola corpora et audiuntur tantum soni. Secundum celum est ubi non corpora uel soni sunt sed corporum et sonorum similitudines. Tercium celum est ubi nec corporum uel sonorum similitudines sunt sed mera et perspicua ueritas. A summo celo Paulus, a medio uero Ysaias et Iohannes canendi formam ad infimum celum detulerunt, et quod angelos canentes audierant ecclesiam canere docuerunt. /

Ezechiel quoque ad medium celum raptus est, ibi quatuor *3r* illa uidit animalia que et plenius quam Iohannes describit, sed eorum minime canticum exprimit. Refert tamen sic: *Audiui post me uocem commotionis magne, 'Benedicta gloria Domini de loco suo,' et uocem alarum animalium percutientium alteram ad alteram.* Hec sane uerba prophetica subtilius inspecta atque discussa utrumque nobis ecclesiasticum canticum innuunt, scilicet, *Gloria Patri et Filio et Spiritui Sancto, Benedicamus Patrem et Filium cum Sancto Spiritu.* Angelos proculdubio propheta in spiritu audiuit canentes, *Benedicta gloria Domini de loco suo.* Quis est locus glorie Domini, id est, creatricis

189 *Pater…operor*: Io 5:17.

194–195 *Sanctus…omnipotens*: Apoc 4:8.

199-204 *Nempe…ueritas*: cf. Augustine, *De Genesi ad litteram libri duodecim* 12.6 (CSEL 28.1, pp 386–387; PL 34:1028–1029).

205 *ad…detulerunt*: i.e. in so far as they record their visionary experiences, Paul, Isaiah, and John convey the form of what they heard to us, who inhabit the first or lowest heaven; cf. the note on lines 104–107 above.

208 *animalia…describit*: cf. Ez 1:5–13.

209–212 *Audiui…alteram*: Ez 3:12–13.

Trinitatis, nisi creatura? Quippe omnis creatura dat gloriam Deo, sua quadam trinitate eius insinuans Trinitatem.

Attende creaturam, et si habes aures audiendi, audi quid canat. Considera omnem creaturam de nichilo conditam, pulchram, et bonam. Quis potuit de nichilo facere nisi omnipotens? Et quis tam pulcra fecit nisi summe sapiens? Et quis tam bona fecit nisi summe bonus? Itaque omnis creatura, eo ipso quo ex nichilo condita sui conditoris potentiam, eo ipso quo pulcra sui formatoris sapientiam, eo ipso quo bona eiusdem insinuat et predicat bonitatem, atque ita sua quadam trinitate creatoris laudat Trinitatem. Nonne hoc est canere, *Gloria Patri et Filio et Spiritui Sancto*? Familiare siquidem est ecclesie catholice nomine potentie personam Patris, nomine sapientie personam Filii, nomine bonitatis designare personam Spiritus Sancti. Si ergo diligenter intendas et subtiliter audias, nichil aliud locus glorie Domini, id est creatura, canit nisi, *Gloria Patri et Filio*

219 *sua…trinitate*: in his assertion that every creature has a trinity of its own, bespeaking the Trinity that created it, William anticipates the next major section of his sermon. He will go on to suggest that every creature has three qualities that each gesture toward a specific Person of the Trinity: its creation or existence (indicating the *potentia Dei* or Father), its beauty (indicating the *sapientia Dei* or Son), and its goodness (indicating the *bonitas Dei* or Holy Ghost). For the association of these qualities with the three Persons, see the note on lines 229–231 below. A similar phrase will recur when William discusses the trinity of human praise for God (i.e. with voice, thought, and action) in line 467.

220 *si…audi*: cf. Mt 11:15, 13:9; Mc 4:9, 4:23, 7:16; Lc 8:8, 14:35.

224–228 *Itaque…Trinitatem*: the main verbs of the first clause, *insinuat et predicat* (lines 226–227), should be supplied following *sui conditoris potentiam* (line 225) and *sui formatoris sapientiam* (line 226).

227 *sua…trinitate*: cf. lines 219 and 467.

229–231 *Familiare…Sancti*: the association of *potentia*, *sapientia*, and *bonitas* with the three Persons of the Trinity was popular in twelfth-century theological writing, especially as the theme was developed in the works of Peter Abelard. See, e.g., Abelard's *Theologia Christiana* 1.4–1.53 (CCCM 12, pp 73–94); see also Hugh of St.-Victor, *De sacramentis Christianae fidei* 1.3.26 (PL 176:227c).

232–233 *locus…Domini*: cf. Ez 3:12.

233 Patri *L* : *omitted by R*

et Spiritui Sancto. Et hoc utique tanto tibi grandius intonat, quanto mens tua tam bone considerationi propensius inuigilat, ut et tu cum propheta non iam uocem lenem sed uocem audias commotionis magne, *Benedicta gloria Domini de loco suo.*

Quod autem sequitur, *Et uocem alarum animalium percutientium alteram ad alteram*, ad rationalem specialiter pertinet creaturam per quatuor animalia significatam. Que nimirum, dum immissarum temptationum incursus fortiter superat, leo est. Dum infirmitatem suam humiliter agnoscit et confitetur, homo est. Dum per carnis mortificationem Deo se offert sacrificium in odorem suauitatis, uitulus est. Dum celestia meditando que sursum sunt sapit, non que super terram, aquila est. Hec, dum pia consideratione intendit in opera Dei ut in his que facta sunt factorem ueneretur atque miretur, audit post se uocem, *Benedicta gloria Domini de loco suo*, id est pie intuetur quomodo ille quoque creature, quas ipsa dignitatis merito antecedit sua illa trinitate, quam superius distinximus, creatrici Trinitati dent gloriam et suo modo dicant, *Gloria Patri et Filio et Spiritui Sancto.*

Et hec est uox commotionis magne, quia rationalem creaturam pie considerantem uehementer commouet et accendit ad canendas Deo laudes. Atque ita illa uox commotionis / magne *3v*
elicit et excitat uocem alarum animalium percutientium alteram ad alteram. Siquidem animalia alas suas alteram ad alteram percutiunt, quando sancti uiri quicquid in se uirtutis est in laudem Dei excitant, seseque inuicem cohortantur uerbo uel exemplo dicentes. Ecce quomodo ab omni creatura creatrici Trinitati laus canitur, atque omnis creature quodammodo generalis uox est: *Gloria Patri et Filio et Spiritui Sancto.* Et certe uox omnis creature debet in nobis esse uox commotionis magne. Nos ergo

237 *Benedicta…suo*: Ez 3:12.

238–239 *Et…alteram*: Ez 3:13.

240–243 *Que…est*: cf. Gregory, *Homiliae in Hiezechihelem prophetam* 1.4.2 (CCSL 142, p. 48; PL 76:815–816). The antecedent of *Que* is *creatura.*

243–244 *Deo…suauitatis*: cf. Eph 5:2

249–250 *quas…distinximus*: cf. William's discussion in the preceding paragraph and the notes on lines 219 and 229–231 above.

ad imaginem eiusdem creatricis Trinitatis conditi atque eius tam crebra, tam preclara beneficia experti, minime sileamus, sed clamemus fortiter et iugiter, *Sanctus, Sanctus, Sanctus, Dominus Deus omnipotens*, id est, *Benedicamus Patrem et Filium cum Sancto Spiritu*. Sic igitur cum propheta dicit, *Audiui post me uocem commotionis magne, 'Benedicta gloria Domini de loco suo,' et uocem alarum animalium percutientium alteram ad alteram*, utrumque ecclesiasticum innuitur canticum, per uocem scilicet commotionis magne, *Gloria Patri et Filio et Spiritui Sancto*, et per uocem alarum animalium percutientium alteram ad alteram, *Benedicamus Patrem et Filium cum Sancto Spiritu*.

Et primum quidem uidetur generale esse canticum omnis creature, secundum uero solius creature rationalis. Quippe si mundum consideres et de creatore interroges, quid aliud respondet quam, 'Deus Trinitas est,' quid aliud tibi canit quam, *Gloria Patri et Filio et Spiritui Sancto*? Interrogatio tua, consideratio tua; responsio eius, species eius. Cum enim figmentum consideras, de figulo interrogas. Et tunc tibi figmentum respondet de figulo, cum ex specie figmenti cognoscis sapientiam figuli. Numquid dicit figmentum ei qui se finxit, id est creatura creatori, 'Quid me fecisti sic?' Quod utique per suam speciem diceret, siquid corruptionis aut feditatis ex fictione, id est creatione, haberet. Nunc autem nichil habet figmentum dicere figulo nisi, 'Gloria tibi qui me fecisti sic. Nam ex nichilo me finxisti, quod est potentie; pulchrum me fecisti, quod est sapientie; bonum me finxisti, quod est bonitatis.' Hoc quidem te audiente, O homo, si habeas aures audiendi, dicit figmentum figulo, id est creatura creatori. Tibi autem quid loquitur, tibi quid aliud quam creatricem predicat Trinitatem, in tuis auribus quid canit, nisi quod sepius dictum est, scilicet, *Gloria Patri et Filio et Spiritui Sancto*?

266–267 *Sanctus…omnipotens*: Apoc 4:8.
282 *figulo*: 'potter'; cf. Ps 2:9b.
283–284 *Numquid…sic*: cf. Rom 9:20, Is 45:9.
290 *si…audiendi*: cf. Mt 11:15, 13:9; Mc 4:9, 4:23, 7:16; Lc 8:8, 14:35.

284 creatori *L* : creatora *R*

Hanc uocem uniuersalis creature tu, O homo, id est creatura rationalis, cum audis, id est cum ex consideratione operum Dei potentiam, sapientiam, bonitatem eius intelligis, in laudem creatricis Trinitatis uehementius exardescis et—quoniam te solum huic laudi prout decet canende minus sufficere iudicas—proximum ad collaudandum prouocas. Quod utique cum facis, pulcre et suauiter coram sanctis angelis canis, *Benedicamus Patrem et Filium cum Sancto Spiritu*. Et cum inuicem se homines uerbo et exemplo excitant ad laudandum in suis moribus Deum, tunc proculdubio in auribus Dei et sanctorum angelorum / *4r* fortiter reboat uox alarum animalium percutientium alteram ad alteram, scilicet, *Benedicamus Patrem et Filium cum Sancto Spiritu*.

Sane uniuersalis creatura non solum laudat sed etiam insinuat creatorem. Rationalis quippe creatura et erudit intellectum et excitat affectum. Erudit intellectum quia ex consideratione operum Dei ad intelligendam creatoris potentiam, sapientiam, bonitatem erudimur, secundum illud Apostoli: *Inuisibilia Dei a creatura mundi per ea que facta sunt intellecta conspiciuntur, sempiterna quoque uirtus eius et diuinitas*. Excitat affectum quia ex consideratione et admiratione operum Dei ad amandum et laudandum artificem Deum excitamur. Sic ergo omnis creatura creatricem non tantum insinuat sed etiam laudat Trinitatem, in altero quidem quodammodo dicens, 'Deus Trinitas est,' in altero uero quodammodo canens, *Gloria Patri et Filio et Spiritui Sancto*.

Sed queritur qua ratione hymnus trium puerorum non tantum bruta sed etiam inanimata hortetur atque inuitet ad laudandum et benedicendum Deum, *Benedicite*, inquiens, *omnia opera Domini Domino, laudate et superexaltate eum in secula*. Et ne quis hoc stricte de sola rationalis creature uni-

312–314 *Inuisibilia…diuinitas*: Rom 1:20.

323–325 *Benedicite…secula*: Dan 3:57. For the liturgical use of this canticle, not listed in CAO, see P. Bernard, 'Le cantique des trois enfants (Dan iii, 52–90): les répertoires liturgiques occidentaux dans l'antiquité tardive et le haut Moyen Age,' *Musica e storia* 1 (1993) 231–272.

313 conspiciuntur *L* : conspicuuntur *R* **322** hortetur : hortatur *RL*

uersitate intelligendum putaret, *Benedicite*, inquit, *imber et ros Domino*, et cetera. Et Dauid in Psalmo, *Laudate*, inquit, *Dominum de terra dracones et omnes abyssi, ignis, grando, nix, glacies, spiritus procellarum*, et cetera. Quomodo hec et huiusmodi laudent Deum—nam omnis creatura laudat creatorem—manifestum est. Hoc enim non est aliud quam rationalem creaturam ex eorum consideratione ad laudandum Deum excitari. Sed quare iubentur laudare siue monentur, cum ad ea non pertineat, siue ex eorum consideratione ad laudandum excitentur homines, siue non excitentur? Respondemus quia cum dicitur, *Benedicite omnia opera Domini Domino*, uel aliquid huiusmodi, nequaquam res brute et inanimate ad benedicendum inuitantur, sed homines sub earum rerum allocutione, quarum consideratione ad benedicendum excitari debent, ad easdem propensius considerandas ut excitentur quodam locutionis genere prouocantur.

Sensus ergo talis est: *Benedicite omnia opera Domini Domino*, id est tu, creatura rationalis, propter quam fecit Deus cetera, cuncta eius opera contemplare, et pia operum contemplatione ad laudandam artificis potentiam, sapientiam, bonitatem excitare. Vnde Dauid in Psalmo cum dixisset, *Benedicite Domino omnia opera eius*, quid in hoc significare uoluerit consequenter aperuit, *In omni*, inquiens, *loco dominationis eius, benedic*

326–327 *Benedicite...Domino*: Dan 3:64.

327–329 *Laudate...procellarum*: Ps 148:7–8.

329–341 *Quomodo...prouocantur*: the idea that 'irrational and inanimate' creatures should excite rational creatures, i.e. human beings, to the praise of God by keeping them mindful of the creator was a common motif in twelfth-century writing, particularly in contemplative, monastic texts. This relationship is discussed at length by Bernard of Clairvaux, *Sermones in Cantica Canticorum* 5 (PL 183:798–803). William adapts this motif in lines 340–341 (*ad easdem...prouocantur*) to correspond to his earlier statement that every creature reflects the triune nature of its creator: the more closely one considers these irrational creatures, the more one should be excited to praise God with very specific songs, i.e. the Trinitarian canticles, as he explains in the subsequent paragraph.

336 *Benedicite...Domino*: Dan 3:57.

346–347 *Benedicite...eius*: Ps 102:22.

348–349 *In...Dominum*: Ps 102:22.

anima mea Dominum. Quasi diceret: Cum dixi, *Benedicite Domino omnia opera eius*, non asino et lapidi locutus sum, sed tibi, O anima mea, ut ex consideratione operum artificem propensius benedicas, atque ita ea que non possunt in se suo creatori benedicant in te. *In omni loco dominationis eius, benedic anima mea Dominum*, id est in omni creatura lauda creatorem. Quod utique non est aliud quam ex omni creatura per piam considerationem diuine colligere laudis materiam.

De origine illius ecclesiastici / cantici, *Benedicamus Pa-* 4v
trem et Filium cum Sancto Spiritu, item illius, *Gloria Patri et Filio et Spiritui Sancto*, hec dicta sufficiant. Restat nunc dicere qualiter a filiis Christiane pietatis cantari debeant. Magis enim cantantur affectu cordis quam strepitu oris. Nam quod de sanctis dicitur, *Exultationes Dei in gutture eorum*, non tantum de gutture carnis accipiendum est. Habet et anima guttur suum quo clamat ad Deum, quo exultat in Deum, secundum illud: *Cor meum et caro mea exultauerunt in Deum uiuum.* Non tantum cor meum sed et caro mea, non tantum caro mea sed et cor meum exultauerunt in Deum uiuum. Nam si plenum est laudibus Dei guttur cordis, impleat necesse est pro loco et tempore guttur carnis, secundum illud dominicum: *Ex habundantia cordis os loquitur.*

Ecce, conueniunt fratres in ecclesiam; incipitur opus Dei. Audis quosdam plenis uocibus et totis uiribus canentes, sicut scriptum est de Dauid, quod totis uiribus saltabat ante Dominum; audis etiam quosdam extenuatis uocibus remisse molliterque canentes et, ut ait quidam, 'Rancidulum quiddam

362 *Exultationes…eorum*: Ps 149:6.
365 *Cor…uiuum*: cf. Ps 83:3.
369–370 *Ex…loquitur*: Mt 12:34, Lc 6:45.
373–374 *totis…Dominum*: 2 Sam 6:14.
375–376 *Rancidulum…loquentes*: cf. A. Persius Flaccus, *Satura* 1:33 (ed. C.F. Hermann, p. 2); Jerome, *Epistola* 54.5 (CSEL 54, p. 471; PL 22:551). Though Persius was read in the Middle Ages, the subject 'quidam' suggests that William most likely knew this quotation only by way of Jerome. William has modified his source, making *loquentes* (line 376) parallel to *canentes* (line 375), while Jerome has 'locuta' and Persius 'locutus.' *Rancidulum* here means 'a putrid stench.'

balba de nare loquentes.’ Nonne statim apud temetipsum de utrisque iudicium celebras, nonne sicut audis iudicas? Audis illos sic, hos uero sic canentes foris. Nonne iudicas eodem modo hos uel illos canere intus, si tamen dicendi sunt canere qui canunt molliter et tepide? Vtinam non canerent, utinam silerent. Nam tepido dicitur: *Vtinam calidus esses aut frigidus, sed quia tepidus es, incipiam te euomere ex ore meo*. Itaque guttur mentis pro mensura impletionis sue implet pro loco et tempore laudibus Dei guttur carnis. Vnde enim ueniunt laudes Dei in guttur carnis, nisi ex gutture mentis? Ex habundantia enim carnis os loquitur siue bonum siue malum. Laudes Dei apud se mens concipit, per os uero parit.

Cor, inquit, *meum et caro mea exultauerunt in Deum uiuum*. Cor meum prius, et consequenter os meum, atque ita communiter cor meum et caro mea exultauerunt in Deum uiuum, id est hilariter atque uiuaciter laudes Dei cecinerunt. Nota ‘hilariter’ in eo quod dicit, *Exultauerunt*, nota ‘uiuaciter’ in eo quod dicit, *Deum uiuum*. Non enim Deo uiuo uoce semimortua mentis uel carnis canendum est. Et quoniam scriptum est, *Seruite Domino in leticia*, exultandum in eum, id est hylari deuocione illi canendum est. Nam sicut hylarem datorem ita etiam hilarem cantorem diligit Deus. Qualem autem diligit, talem et exigit siue datorem siue cantorem. Cum ergo de sanctis dicitur, *Exultationes Dei in gutture eorum*, non tantum guttur carnis sed multo magis guttur mentis, per quod guttur carnis impletur, intellige—porro exultationes Dei nichil aliud quam laudes Deo hilariter decantatas. Qui enim laudat eum minus

376 *balba de nare*: ‘from a lisping nose,’ i.e. ‘with a lisp and nasally.’

378–380 *Nonne...tepide*: ‘Do you not likewise judge the interior singing of the latter or the former—if those who sing feebly and quietly can be said to sing at all?’

381–382 *Vtinam...meo*: Apoc 3:15–16. Cf. the quotation and exegesis of this verse in William’s homily on Lc 11:27, lines 608–609.

383 *guttur mentis*: Gregory, *Homiliae in Evangelia* 1.15.3 (CCSL 141, p. 106; PL 76:1133a).

385–386 *Ex...loquitur*: cf. Mt 12:34, Lc 6:45.

388 *Cor...uiuum*: cf. Ps 83:3.

394–395 *Seruite...leticia*: Ps 99:2.

399 *Exultationes...eorum*: Ps 149:6.

deuote, etsi / laudes Dei, non tamen exultationes Dei, habet in *5r*
gutture.

Sunt autem quidam laudes Dei studiose et totis uiribus canentes, non tamen sincere, sed uel humani fauoris uel commodi temporalis gratia. Hii plane inaniter strepunt, atque aerem fortiter uerberantes in Dei laudibus fiunt ad Deum uelut es sonans aut cimbalum tinniens. Laudes enim Dei, sed non Deo, canunt. Sibi potius laudes Dei canunt, uel illi rei cuius amore canunt. *Reddite*, inquit Dominus, *que sunt Cesaris Cesari et que sunt Dei Deo*. De parte huius precepti que ad Cesarem pertinet ipsi uiderint, sed incunctanter dixerim quia precipuam eiusdem precepti partem, que scilicet ad Deum pertinet, minime obseruant. Non enim Deo que Dei sunt reddunt, qui laudes quidem Dei, sed non Deo, canunt. Non ergo in Dei laudibus bene os strepit, nisi quando ex animi pietate quod canitur in buccam uenit, nisi quando interior cytharedus, id est pius hilarisque in Deum affectus, ad eliciendos sonos dulcissimos cordas lingue et gutturis tangit.

Denique uox talis magis attribuenda est cytharedo quam cythare, id est affectui quam gutturi, iuxta illud Iohannis in Apocalipsi: *Et uocem*, inquit, *quam audiui, quasi cytharedorum cytharizantium in cytharis suis*. Non ait, 'Vocem quasi cythararum,' sed, *Vocem*, inquit, *quasi cytharedorum*, utique elicientium articulatos sonos ex cytharis, unde et addit, *Cytharizantium in cytharis suis*. Et nota quod non ait simpliciter, 'In cytharis,' sed, *In cytharis*, inquit, *suis*. Nam piis animis sua cuique cythara est ad canendas Deo laudes, gutturis et oris officium.

Ingressus ecclesiam, audis fratres psallentes non tantum suauiter sed etiam iuxta propheticam admonitionem sapienter, seruantes scilicet—quod non modice constat esse uirtutis—in

408–409 *uelut…tinniens*: 1 Cor 13:1.

411–412 *Reddite…Deo*: Mt 22:21; cf. Lc 20:25.

423–424 *Et…suis*: Apoc 14:2.

428–430 *Nam…officium*: the phrase *gutturis et oris officium* explains the use of *cuique* in line 429, i.e. 'Among pious souls there is a harp proper [*sua*] to each, the office of the throat and the office of the mouth.'

431–432 *psallentes…sapienter*: cf. Ps 46:8.

sua hilaritate grauitatem, in sua grauitate hilaritatem. Audis, inquam, eos graui hilaritate atque hilari grauitate Domino modulantes et dulcedinem armonie celestis canoris uocibus pro modulo suo imitantes. Mirum si non tanta suauitate uehementer afficeris, si non multum alliceris. Ergo hinc exiens dices, 'Fui in ecclesia, ibique audiui uocem quasi cytharedorum cytharizantium in citharis suis,' id est uocem piorum cordium per gutturis et oris officium Deo laudes debita deuotione canentium.

Liquet igitur laudes Deo magis cantari pio et hylari affectu cordis quam sonoro strepitu oris. Quid enim est in laudibus Dei uocis officium, nisi pii cordis organum? Denique sine oris strepitu Deo pro tempore laudabiliter solo cantatur affectu; porro sine affectu cordis inanis est strepitus oris. Sane quod ait Salomon, *Tempus loquendi et tempus tacendi*, etiam in Dei laudibus ad corporalis uocis officium pertinet. Nam propter huius uite necessitates plurimas et cotidianas minus temporis aptari potest diuinis laudibus uel sup/pressa uoce canendis. *5v* Animi autem affectus plus temporis habet ad canendas Deo laudes. Nam plerumque dum a laudibus diuinis cogitur silere os carnis, Deo cantat os cordis. At propter tam multa uite huius negocia auocantia mentem in aliud, propter multiplices huius temporis necessitates inbecillem animum miserabiliter dilaniantes, nec ipse affectus iugiter laudibus potest diuinis uacare. Quid est ergo quod dicit Propheta, *Benedicam Dominum in omni tempore*? Et quasi parum dixisset, adiunxit, *Semper laus eius in ore meo*. Si de ore carnis hoc accipis, tam sepe in quolibet a diuinis laudibus clauditur. Si uero de ore mentis, ipsum quoque etiam in homine apostolice siue prophetice perfectionis plerumque, immo sepe, a diuinis silere laudibus cogitur, dum

447 *Tempus…tacendi*: cf. Eccl 3:7.

457–459 *Benedicam…meo*: cf. Ps 33:2.

459–464 *Si…cogitantem*: William suggests that, like continual vocal praise of God, continual mental or intentional praise of God is impossible in this life, even for those as close to perfection as Paul or David. This observation will lead him to posit the third element of his trinity of human praise, i.e. praise expressed in one's actions or way of life. The phrase *immo sepe* is meant to clarify or intensify *plerumque* ('sometimes, nay, rather quite frequently…'). *Ipsum*, the subject of *cogitur*, refers to the *os mentis*.

corpus corruptibile aggrauat animam, et deprimit terrena habitatio sensum multa cogitantem.

Quomodo ergo ait Propheta, *Semper laus eius in ore meo*? Questio non modica est, cui soluende pro uiribus intendamus. Creatricem Trinitatem quadam nostra trinitate laudare debemus. Non enim solummodo affectu cordis et sono gutturis, sed etiam perseuerantia pie conuersationis illi canendum est. Canat illi mens nostra, canat uox nostra, canat uita nostra: et tunc uere a nobis creatrix laudatur Trinitas, tunc uere a nobis canitur, *Gloria Patri et Filio et Spiritui Sancto*. Verum sic est animus ut arcus. Non potest arcus diu esse tensus, nec animus diu potest esse intensus. Non ergo mens nostra diuinis potest laudibus intendere iugiter. Multo minus uox nostra iugi sufficit laudationi. Sed ecce silet uox cordis, silet uox carnis; numquid silere debet uox pie conuersationis? Lassatur animus, lassatur caro, sed numquid pium lassatur propositum? Quamdiu in bono proposito perseueras, in tuis moribus Deum laudas. Quamdiu in te pie conuersationis status non uacillat, proculdubio uite tue sinceritas Deum laudare non cessat. Si a uite munditia deficis, a Dei laudibus obmutescis. Hoc significauit Dauid cum diceret, *Benedicam Dominum in omni tempore*. Nempe hoc est quod ait Iob, *Iustificationem meam quam cepi tenere non deseram*. Qui enim iustificationem suam quam cepit tenere non deserit, pii propositi perseuerancia Deum in omni tempore benedicit. Quod ergo adiungitur, *Semper laus eius in ore meo*, neque de ore cordis neque de ore carnis sed de ore, ut ita dicam, pie conuersationis intelligendum est, quo nimirum Deus, etiam ore carnis clauso et corde circa temporalium dispositionem occupato, preclare plurimumque laudatur. Hoc modo soluitur et illud Apostoli: *Sine intermissione orate*. Quippe in electis et cum lingua non orat, animus non orat, uita orat, eo ipso orare non desinens quo in sua sinceritate persistens.

465 *Semper…meo*: Ps 33:2.
467 *quadam…trinitate*: cf. lines 219 and 227.
483 *Benedicam…tempore*: Ps 33:2.
484 *Iustificationem…deseram*: Iob 27:6.
487 *Semper…meo*: Ps 33:2.
492 *Sine…orate*: 1 Thess 5:17.

Sciendum uero quod et ipsa uita Christiana quandam in se propriam habet trinitatem, qua creatricem iugiter benedicit Trinitatem. Illam sane uite Christiane trinitatem magnus Christiane sapientie puteus, Paulum dico, insinuans, *Sobrie*, inquit, *et iuste, et pie uiuamus in hoc seculo, expectantes beatam spem.* Itaque uita Christiana cum tenax est sobrietatis, iusticie, / pietatis, sua trinitate laudes creatricis canit Trinitatis. *6r* Sobrie debemus uiuere ad nosmetipsos, iuste ad proximum, pie ad Deum. Sobrietatem ad nosmetipsos tenere debemus duobus modis, scilicet ne in sensu nostro plus iusto habundemus, iuxta illud Apostoli: *Non plus sapere quam oportet sapere, sed sapere ad sobrietatem*, et ne ex calice Babilonis carnalium desideriorum uino debriemur, iuxta illud eiusdem Apostoli: *Carnis curam ne feceritis in desideriis*. Iusticiam quoque ad proximum tenere debemus, ut scilicet eadem mensura qua nobis metimur et proximo metiamur, iuxta illud dominicum: *Quecumque uultis ut uobis faciant homines et uos similiter facite illis.* Sic enim illud quo nichil est equius preceptum implemus: *Diliges proximum tuum sicut te ipsum.* Pietatem uero ad Deum tenere debemus, que scilicet, ut ait pater Augustinus, Grece dicitur 'Theosebian,' id est bonus cultus. Huius nimirum exprimit formulam maximum illud primumque preceptum, scilicet: *Diliges Dominum Deum tuum ex toto corde tuo, et ex tota anima tua, et ex tota mente tua, et ex omnibus uiribus tuis*. Non enim ut decet pietas a nobis ad Deum seruatur, nisi totum quod ab eo accepimus illi per amoris puritatem refundatur. Sic ergo uiuendo, id est tenendo ad nosmetipsos sobrietatem, ad proximum iusticiam, ad Deum pietatem, hac laudabili uite nostre trinitate

498 *puteus*: cf. line 12 above.
498–500 *Sobrie...spem*: Tit 2:12–13.
505–506 *Non...sobrietatem*: Rom 12:3.
506 *calice Babilonis*: cf. Ier 51:7, Apoc 16:19.
507–508 *Carnis...desideriis*: Rom 13:14.
510–511 *Quecumque...illis*: cf. Mt 7:12, Lc 6:31.
512–513 *Diliges...ipsum*: Mt 19:19, 22:39, Gal 5:14, Iac 2:8; cf. Mc 12:31, Lc 10:27, Rom 13:9.
514–515 *Grece...Theosebian*: Augustine, *De Trinitate* 12.14.22 (CCSL 50, p. 375; PL 42:1010). The Greek word is Θεοσέβεια.
516–518 *Diliges...tuis*: cf. Mt 22:37, Mc 12:30, Lc 10:27, Deut 6:5.

creatricem prout decet benedicimus Trinitatem, scilicet Patrem et Filium cum Sancto Spiritu.

Sunt autem hec tria, sobrietas, iusticia, pietas, in uita uere Christiani ita connexa, ut a se disiungi non possint. Quippe pietas, id est Dei cultus, iusticiam exigit, que ad proximum seruanda est. Vnde premisso maximo et primo precepto, scilicet, *Diliges Dominum Deum tuum ex toto corde, tota anima, tota mente*, consequenter annexum est, *Et proximum tuum sicut te ipsum*. Et non solum iusticiam, que ad proximum seruanda est, sed etiam sobrietatem, quam ad nosmetipsos tenere debemus, pietas, id est Dei cultus, in tantum exigit ut uoce terribili Apostolus intonet, *Qui autem sunt Christi, carnem suam crucifixerunt cum uiciis et concupiscentiis*. Quia igitur uita bona his tribus uel aliquo horum trium numquam carere potest, iccirco Propheta cui cordi erat bene, id est sobrie et iuste et pie, uiuere; *Benedicam*, inquit, *Dominum in omni tempore, semper laus eius in ore meo*. Quasi diceret: Et lingua silente, que utique iugi laudationi non sufficit, et corde per aliquam occupationem in aliud auocato, uita mea laudabit Dominum, eo ipso iugi laudationi sufficiens, quo a sua sobrietate, iusticia, et pietate non deficiens, eo ipso creatricem Trinitatem, scilicet Patrem et Filium cum Sancto Spiritu iugiter benedicens, quo suam trinitatem in tantis uite huius periculis caute firmiterque custodiens.

Et sciendum quia uita uere Christiani non tantum in se Deum laudat, sed etiam alios ad collaudandum excitat, secundum illud: *Videant opera uestra bona, et glorificent Patrem uestrum qui in celis est*. Vtrumque ergo canticum cantat, scilicet, *Gloria Patri et Filio et Spiritui Sancto*, et, *Benedicamus Patrem et Filium cum Sancto Spiritu*. Quippe in eo quod Deum, id est omnipotentem Trinitatem, in se laudat, *Gloria Patri et Filio et Spiritui Sancto* suauiter personat. / Porro in eo quod alios ad *6v*

523–524 *benedicimus…Spiritu*: cf. CAO 6238/7966.
529–530 *Diliges…mente*: cf. Mt 22:37, Mc 12:30, Lc 10:27, Deut 6:5.
530–531 *Et…ipsum*: Lc 10:27; cf. Mt 22:37, Mc 12:30.
534–535 *Qui…concupiscentiis*: Gal 5:24.
537 *Propheta…bene*: cf. 3 Reg 8:18.
538–539 *Benedicam…meo*: Ps 33:2.
548–549 *Videant…est*: Mt 5:16.

collaudandum et conbenedicendum excitat, *Benedicamus Patrem et Filium cum Sancto Spiritu* sollempniter concrepat.

O cantica suauia atque salubria, et cantantibus tanto salubriora, quanto et suauiora! Nichil his salubrius canitur, immo nichil aliud salubriter canitur. Nam quid aliud canit tota uita iustorum? Sed nec aliud canit beata illa uita angelorum. Nam quod illi salubriter, hoc isti canunt feliciter. Et quidem in illa regione uiuorum nichil aliud canitur; porro in hac ualle miserie, ubi non tantum grana sunt sed etiam palee, a granis quidem nichil aliud canitur, a paleis uero aliud canitur, sed tanto utique pernitiosius, quanto suauius. Vnde de Babilone sub typo omnium impiorum dicitur: *Quantum glorificauit se, et in deliciis fuit, tantum date illi tormentum et luctum.* Igitur ab angelis in celo et ab electis hominibus in terra idem canitur, scilicet, *Gloria Patri et Filio et Spiritui Sancto*; pure tamen celeste est canticum et non terrenum. Nam etsi pro tempore canatur in terra, non tamen est de terra, quia desursum uenit. Et in quantum canitur in terra, in tantum terrenos facit celestes. Vnde magnus ille cantici huius precentor in terra: *Nostra*, inquit, *conuersatio in celis est.* Verum nunc in terra subrauce ab hominibus canitur, suo tempore canendum ab hominibus sicut ab angelis, quando scilicet humilitas hominum iuxta promissionem Saluatoris ad equalitatem sublimabitur angelorum. Per eundem Dominum nostrum Ihesum Christum, qui cum Patre et Spiritu Sancto uiuit et regnat, Deus per omnia secula seculorum. Amen.

560–561 *in…uiuorum*: cf. Ps 114:9
561–562 *non…palee*: cf. Lc 3:17.
565–566 *Quantum…luctum*: Apoc 18:7.
572 *Nostra…est*: Phil 3:20.

577 Ihesum Christum *L* : *omitted in R*

II Omelia super Cum loqueretur Ihesus ad turbas

Edited from

Oxford, Bodleian Library, MS Rawlinson C. 31, fols 7r–13v

OMELIA SUPER CUM LOQUERETUR IHESUS AD TURBAS

Cum loqueretur Ihesus ad turbas, extollens uocem quedam 7r
mulier de turba dixit illi, 'Beatus uenter qui te portauit et ubera que suxisti.'

I

Expulerat misericors Dominus a misero homine demonium, secundum Lucam mutum, secundum Matheum etiam surdum. Insigne hoc opus duo eque insignia consecuta sunt. Quippe expulso demonio surdus recepit auditum, mutus eloquium. Turbis pro signo triplici admirantibus, uerentes scribe et pharisei ne forte admiratio pareret uenerationem quod inficiari quia sollempne erat non poterant sinistra interpretatione inficere laborabant, mira cecitate uel pocius malignitate allegantes quod in Beelzebub principe demoniorum eiceret demonia. Eorum uero uel erranti ignorantie uel mentienti malicie tam uiuaciter et tam acute a Domino responsum est, ut uirus quod asperserant ad corrumpendam audientis populi simplicitatem infirmum atque inefficax redderetur. Suo nimirum exemplo magistra nos Veritas docuit ut si quando homines—quia ueris non possunt—

2–4 *Cum...suxisti*: Lc 11:27. The verse appears here as it would when Lc 11:27–28 was read as the Gospel of the day, i.e., with the addition of the non-biblical introductory phrase *Cum...turbas*. See the Introduction, p. 14, n. 39. Subsequent quotations of this verse will not be noted.

5–6 *demonium...surdum*: cf. Lc 11:14, Mt 9:32.

9–12 *uerentes...laborabant*: the clause *ne...uenerationem* is the object of *uerentes*, while the clause *quod...poterant* is the object of *inficere laborabant*: 'they [the Scribes and Pharisees] laboured to contaminate with a sinister interpretation what they were unable to deny, since it was profound ...'

12 *pocius*: the orthography of the second sermon in Rawlinson is inconsistent: sometimes, as here, the scribe writes 'ci' for a soft 'ti', while elsewhere he does not observe this distinction.

13 *in...demonia*: Lc 11:15.

1 OMELIA...TURBAS *supplied from a list of contents on fol. 2v S : omitted by R : omitted by L, which here reads* Sermo in vigilia asumptionis Sancte Marie, de Euangelica lectione

falsis nos ceperint infamare criminibus, ea nequaquam nostra taciturnitate nutriamus, sed pocius sapientis eloquii libertate cum modestia et tranquillitate diluamus. Cum ergo Dominus contra malignantes et calumpniantes nequaquam pro potestate indignaretur, sed pocius crimen ab eis obiectum modesta ratione diluere dignaretur, in altero pacientie, in altero uero sapientie formam dans suis, in persona unius muliercule insigniter declaratum est quod alio loco Patri dicit, *Abscondisti hec a sapientibus et prudentibus, et reuelasti ea paruulis.*

Sic enim noster Lucas contexit: *Factum est autem cum hec diceret, extollens uocem quedam mulier de turba dixit illi, 'Beatus uenter qui te portauit et ubera que suxisti.'* Tam multi uiri erant in turba; tacentibus uniuersis una mulier eructauit uerbum bonum, uerbum dulce nimis. Infirma enim mundi eligit Deus ut confundat forcia. Sane in hac muliere quatuor precipue sunt notanda, laudanda, imitanda, scilicet prudencia, fides, fiducia, deuocio. Acutam eius prudenciam intuere. Sublimia et mistica Dominus loquebatur et pluebat super peccatores laqueos, super pios uero auditores salutaris doctrine imbrem. Et ceteri quidem pie audientes eum ut sapientem hominem audiebant; una mulier aperiens os suum et fortius attrahens spiritum uerba loquentis acutius altiusque inspexit et Deum loqui intellexit. Signum dominicum uiderat / et contra blasphemantes *7v*
uerbum disserentis audiebat. Prudenter ergo aduertens signum pariter et uerbum, misterii latentis inuenit thesaurum. Denique per sapientiam loquentis cognouit potentiam facientis. Cognouit ex redditis ab illo rationibus quod in spiritu Dei imperaret demonibus. Sed et ex hoc creuit ad maius. Cognouit enim quod non posset in spiritu Dei imperare demonibus, si esset purus homo carnaliter natus ex hominibus. Cognouit, inquam,

22–23 *nequaquam... indignaretur*: i.e., Christ did not regard the *malignantes et calumpniantes* with scorn from his position of divine authority (*pro potestate*), but rather he answered them with a rational argument (*modesta ratione*, lines 23–24).

26–27 *Abscondisti...paruulis*: Lc 10:21, Mt 11:25.

32–33 *Infirma...forcia*: 1 Cor 1:27.

33–35 *Sane...deuocio*: cf. Bede, *In Lucam* 4.215–220 (CCSL 120, p. 236; PL 92:479c–d).

36-37 *pluebat..., laqueos*: Ps 10:7.

45–46 *in...demonibus*: cf. Mt 12:28.

quod non posset proprie auctoritatis imperio agere quod sancti plerumque uel orando uel per nomen maius adiurando efficiunt si non esset Deus. Itaque eo ipso quo cognouit eum imperare demonibus in spiritu Dei, cognouit etiam eum ex eodem natum esse spiritu atque esse filium uirginis, quod utique esse non posset nisi esset et filius Dei.

Proinde illi taliter acclamauit, *Beatus uenter qui te portauit et ubera que suxisti*. Vnum refertur ad potentiam facientis, scilicet, *Beatus uenter qui te portauit*, aliud ad sapientiam loquentis, scilicet, *Et ubera que suxisti*. *Beatus*, inquit, *uenter qui te portauit*, qui eicis demonia in spiritu Dei, et hoc imperiose, non per orationem uel alterius nominis adiurationem, eo ipso probans te de eodem natum spiritu et uentre portatum uirgineo. *Et beata ubera que suxisti*, qui tam subtiliter et tam salubriter et tam supra hominem loqueris, eo ipso probans tam sacris te labiis lac suxisse uirgineum. Numquam enim homo simplici imperio, id est sine oratione uel adiuratione, expulit demones ut tu facis, numquam sic locutus est homo ut tu loqueris, eo ipso probans quod ita sis homo uerus, ut non sis homo merus. Nam et Deus es uere, qui sic facis et sic loqueris in homine quem elegisti et assumpsisti. Beatus, plane beatus homo ille, quem, in eo quod Deus es, elegisti et assumpsisti in unitatem persone, et hec beatitudo redundat ad uentrem qui te portauit et ubera que suxisti.

Sic igitur memorabilis mulier ex pio et prudenti auditu creuit ad fidem; nam fides ex auditu, ut ait Apostolus. Quantus autem concepte fidei mox in suis iniciis feruor extiterit, preclara eius fiducia indicat. Non enim uerita multitudinem plebis incredule, non proceres populi quos loquenti Saluatori uidebat infestos, scribas scilicet et phariseos qui clauem scientie et pondus auctoritatis habere uidebantur, ausa quoque supra sexum, nam loqui in concione non est mulierum, extollens uocem dixit, id est pro grandi affectu grandi etiam uoce intonuit, *Beatus uenter*, et cetera. Tanta iam erat eius fiducia pro ipso cuius eam mox

69–72 *Beatus...suxisti*: cf. *Explanatio* 4:5–6 (p. 184).
74 *fides ex auditu*: Rom 10:17.
78 *clauem scientie*: Lc 11:52.
82–83 *Tanta...accenderat: cuius* refers back to *pro ipso*, i.e. Christ, while *eam* refers back to *eius*, i.e. the woman. Read: *mox ut cuius sermo*

ut sermo ad fidem inbuerat, etiam amor ad zelum accenderat. Et non solum preclara pro ipso, sed etiam noua ad ipsum fiducia utebatur, ausa, ut ita dicam, supra humanum modum. Dicit enim alibi Euangelista sacer quod Dominus Ihesus ad populum loquebatur non ut scri/be et pharisei, sed quasi potestatem *8r* habens, atque in uerbis eius nescio quid maiestatis, unde hostes eius terrerentur, apparebat. Denique sermo eius quibus non erat amabilis in tantum erat terribilis ut non possent uel auderent impedire loquentem.

Erant autem in populo qui audiebat eum quidam pii, quidam etiam impii auditores. Et pii quidem auditores uerbis eius suauiter pascebantur, impii uero eisdem grauiter urebantur. Porro nullus uel horum uel illorum ausus est interrumpere uerba loquentis. In tantum sermo eius illis erat reuerencie et honori, in tantum uero istis metui et terrori. Inter pios sane auditores unam mulierem sermo loquentis altius et plenius imbuit, quia maiori pietate audiuit. Hec oblita reuerencie pro impetu deuocionis ausa est interrumpere uerba Domini loquentis. Sic enim ait noster Lucas, *Factum est autem cum hec diceret, extollens uocem quedam mulier de turba*, et cetera. Non ait, 'Cum hec dixisset,' sed, 'Cum hec diceret.' Interrupit ergo sermonem loquentis. Nullus malorum auditorum, quibus nimirum sermo Domini erat grauis, adeo potuit esse demens ut hoc auderet. Non poterat tantum presumere liuor quantum amor. Nam etiam ad presumendum amorem liuore forciorem esse oportet. Verum cum uerba loquentis Domini pie fuerint auditrici tam suauia et sapida ut non posset ea fastidire, quomodo non potuit ea sustinere? Plane uerba loquentis Domini tam dulcia et iocunda

---

eam ad fidem inbuerat, cuius amor eam ad zelum accenderat. The woman's trust in Christ is so great that, at the same time that she is initiated into the Christian faith, she is also illuminated with profound, theologically complicated knowledge, reflected in her statement, *Beatus uenter*, etc.

84–85 *preclara…utebatur*: *preclara* and *noua* are both ablative, modifying *fiducia* as the object of *utebatur*.

86–88 *quod…habens*: cf. Mt 7:29, Mc 1:22, Lc 19:17.

106 *Non…amor*: cf. Augustine, *In Psalmum cxviii Ennaratio* 28.2 and 30.6 (CCSL 40, pp 1761 and 1769; PL 37:1582 and 1590).

107 presumendum *LS* : presummendum *R*

erant pie auditrici quod diu non poterant sustineri. Nempe ex illis pia et prudens auditrix concepit spiritum, qui nimirum adeo uehemens erat ut coartaret eam nimis ad eructandum uerbum bonum, et factus est uenter eius quasi mustum absque spiraculo quod laguncula nouas dirumpit.

Locuta est et respirauit paululum. Eructauit uerbum bonum, dominicum pro impetu sancte deuocionis pio ausu interrumpens eloquium. Sacra ipsa Domini uerba, quibus inbuebatur et ex quibus accendebatur, non poterat diutius sustinere, quia uerbum bonum quod mente conceperat pre magnitudine deuocionis non poterat apud se quin erumperet ulterius continere. Itaque expectare non potuit fortiter exestuans intus deuocio ut Dominus peroraret, sed dum adhuc loquitur, multa ui erupit, mira fiducia, ne dicam audacia, uerba maiestatis interrupit. Preclara quidem eius fiducia in eo quod populum et proceres non est uerita quin publice acclamaret Saluatori, sed preclarior—quia multo inusitatior—in eo quod eundem Dominum maiestatis non est reuerita quin eius interrumperet tam sacra et tam salubria uerba. Illud feruide fidei, hoc flagrantissime deuocionis fuit. Plerumque enim deuotio, id est intensior uis pii amoris, quo plus habet fiducie in dilectum, eo / minus reuerencie habere *8v*
dinoscitur. Inde est quod non est ueritus recumbere in sinu Ihesu discipulus ille, quem se diligentem diligebat Ihesus. Plane ille recubitus minus habuit reuerencie, plus fiducie. Similiter et illa uox pie mulieris sermonem dominicum, dum ei ex multa deuocione acclamat, interrumpere non uerentis. Non imputat ei Dominus hanc interruptionis iniuriam, non arguit quasi ream maiestatis, quam inebriauerat uinum flagrantissime caritatis. Denique tam uehementi eius affectu fortiter attractus atque illectus, omittit loqui populo quem indeuotio faciebat uerbis eius indignum, atque ad eam conuersus non tantum eam blande

111–116 *Nempe…paululum*: cf. Iob 32:18–20a. Here William frames a nearly verbatim quotation of Iob 32:19 (*uenter…dirumpit*) with allusions to the preceding and subsequent verses. Before the quotation, his diction is guided in part by Iob 32:18; following the quotation, he adapts Iob 32:20a.

116 *Eructauit…bonum*: cf. Ps 44:2.

132–133 *Inde…Ihesus*: cf. Io 13:23.

140 *indeuotio*: 'lack of piety or reverence.'

affatur, uerum etiam quod ab ipsa minus dictum est supplere dignatur, *Quin immo*, inquiens, *beati qui audiunt uerbum Dei et custodiunt illud.*

Sane huius mulieris etiam in hoc prudencia notanda est et laudanda, quod Saluatori sollempniter acclamando non tantum ardentissimum affectum, quem in ipsum habebat, eximie declarauit, sed etiam sexum proprium preclare honorauit. Refundit quippe in matrem excellenciam pignoris, dum beatum dicit uentrem gratia tam beati oneris et beata ubera gratia alumpni tam nobilis. Mulierem decus mulierum pia mulier digno effert preconio; cui nimirum dum tam multum largitur, sibi quoque non nichil impertitur. Illius enim mulieris que peperit Saluatorem priuilegium sic habundat, quod in omnem sexum muliebrem ad expiandum dedecus quod prima inuexerat mulier gloriose redundat. Acutius itaque prouidens pia et prudens mulier posse sibi sic obici: 'Unde tibi tantum confidencie uel pocius impudencie, mulier, ut in tantorum cetu uirorum sic exclamare audeas?' in ipsa sua exclamatione uetustum muliebris sexus

143–144 *Quin... illud*: Lc 11:28.

151–153 *Mulierem... impertitur*: the appositive objects *mulierem* and *decus mulierum* refer to Mary, as does *cui*. The subject of *largitur* and *impertitur* is *pia mulier*, i.e. the *mulier* of Lc 11:27. The phrase *non nichil* is an example of litotes.

153–156 *Illius... redundat*: cf. *Explanatio* 7:2 (p. 308, for drinking of the Virgin's excess of grace); 2:1–2 and 7:2 (pp 111 and 307, for the relation between Mary and Eve).

156–157 *providens... obici*: 'foreseeing that objections could thus be made against her'; *pia et prudens mulier* is the subject of *insinuat*, line 161. Defending the female sex through recourse to the Virgin Mary was a common strategy in medieval literature, though, as Alcuin Blamires has noted, its success was limited by two main factors, both present in William's writing. First, the praise of Mary as the supremely good woman was necessarily contrasted with the supremely sinful character of Eve, i.e. the grace given to Mary made up for the anciently rooted frailty of the sex. Second, praising Mary for her role as Christ's mother focused attention on her 'wondrous singularity and singular wondrousness,' to quote Anselm of Bec, setting her apart from the rest of her sex rather than making her in any way comparable to other women. See Blamires, *The Case for Women in Medieval Culture* (Oxford 1998), esp. pp 120–121; as well as the sources collected in *Woman Defamed and Woman Defended: An Anthology of Medieval Texts*, ed. Blamires et al. (Oxford 1992).

dedecus non tantum expiatum, uerum etiam in gloriam commutatum insinuat, pro eo quod hic sexus genuit aluitque Saluatorem, atque inde sibi tantum esse non impudentis audacie, sed libertatis et fiducie, ut eidem Saluatori sublimia disserenti sollempniter acclamare mulier minime uereatur. Vetusti igitur dedecoris expiatricem et sexus muliebris nobilitatricem, eo ipso quo Saluatoris genitricem atque altricem, in filio loquente sublimius quam loqui posset purus hominis filius, mirabilis mulier uenerando admirans et admirando uenerans, *Beatus*, inquit, *uenter qui te portauit et ubera que suxisti.*

Nulla quippe alia mulier hanc beatitudinem cum Dei genitrice communicat siue partitur. Sola lactauit quem de se pure, id est sine uirilis admixtione seminis, generauit. Sicut nullus uirorum potuit illi communicare in tanti filii / generatione, sic nec *9r* aliqua mulierum in eiusdem lactatione. Sicut ergo Saluatoris generatio sue matri est quasi fons proprius cui non communicat alienus, sic et eiusdem lactatio illi est quasi uena propria cui non communicat aliena. Nimirum pius et dulcis Dominus, ut sua genitrix illa uentris et uberum beatitudine sola gauderet, aliam nutricem quam propriam genitricem habere noluit, immo dedignatus est, quia ipsum non decuit. Nam sicut uentre portari uirgineo, sic et ubera uirginea sugere eius fuit. Nasci partu uirgineo, pasci lacte uirgineo, utrumque mirum, utrumque singulare, utrumque decuit uenientem ad operandam salutem in medio terre Dominum glorie. Sic nasci oportuit per quem renasceremur, sic pasci decuit a quo uitaliter pasceremur. Numquid res inusitatior et mirabilior est partus uirgineus quam lac uirgineum? Vna uirgo ab eterno inuenta est in utero habens, et eadem sola inuenta est in pectore lactescens. Vnde in utero habens, inde in pectore lactescens. Vnde inquam illi fetus, inde illi lac. Fetus unde uirgini? Matheum nostrum audi: *Cum desponsata*, inquit, *esset Maria Ioseph, inuenta est in utero habens de Spiritu Sancto*. Ecce, unde fetus uirgini, plane

170–171 *Nulla…partitur*: cf. *Explanatio* 2:4 (p. 118).
171–172 *Sola…generauit*: cf. Bede, *In Lucam* 4.226–234 (CCSL 120, pp 236–237; PL 92:479d–480a).
183–184 *ad…terre*: cf. Ps 73:12.
184–186 *Sic…pasceremur*: cf. *Explanatio* 1:3, 7:4, and 8:10 (pp 88, 310, and 352–353).
191–192 *Cum…Sancto*: Mt 1:18.

inde etiam lac uirgini. Fetus illi de Spiritu Sancto, et pro fetu alendo eque illi lac de Spiritu Sancto.

Opere quippe nature non potuit uirgo lactescere, sicut nec in utero habere. Itaque lac uirgineum eque ut fetus uirgineus supra naturam est, de Spiritu Sancto est, res mira et singularis est. Vnde pia et prudens mulier ad filium uirginis: *Beatus*, inquit, *uenter qui te portauit et ubera que suxisti*. Beatus uenter qui te portauit, quia habens de Spiritu Sancto, et beata ubera que suxisti, quia lactescentia itidem de Spiritu Sancto. Si iccirco beatus uenter qui te portauit quia tumens de Spiritu Sancto, quomodo beata ubera que suxisti, si non tumencia eque de Spiritu Sancto? Nunc autem et beatus ille uenter et beata illa ubera. Beatus ille uenter, quia uirgineus et plenus; beata illa ubera, quia uirginea et plena: ille fetu, hec lacte. Illi fetus de Spiritu Sancto, his lac eque de Spiritu Sancto. Alioquin nec ille uirgineus, nec hec essent uirginea.

Beatus inquam ille uenter non quia uirgineus, nam multi sunt uentres uirginei, nec quia plenus, nam multi sunt uentres pleni, sed quia uirgineus simul et plenus, quod scilicet nullus alius. Et beata illa ubera non quia uirginea, nam multa sunt ubera uirginea, nec quia plena, quia multa sunt ubera plena, sed quia uirginea simul et plena, quod scilicet nulla alia. Non decuit beati uentris fructum nisi beata illa ubera sugere, nec decuit beata illa ubera sugi ab alio. Dedignatus est fetus ille uirgineus pasci lacte non uirgineo, nec fetui non uirgineo potuit—quia non decuit—lac preberi uirgineum. Nam sicut uentrem illum sanctificauerat / sibi Altissimus, ut scilicet neminem portaret *9v* post ipsum, ita et ubera illa sanctificauit sibi, ut scilicet a nemine sugerentur preter ipsum. Plane beatus ille uenter et beata illa ubera. Ille tumens de Spiritu Sancto ad effundendum nobis uite auctorem; hec tumencia eque de Spiritu Sancto ad pascendum nobis uerum pastorem.

Intellexit per Spiritum pia illa exclamatrix altitudinem sacramenti huius, fide intus fortiter estuans, foris autem sollempni

195–197 *Opere…singularis est*: cf. Bede, *In Lucam* 4.231–243 (CCSL 120, pp 236–237; PL 92:479d–480a).

209–224 *Beatus…pastorem*: cf. *Explanatio* 4:10 (p. 197).

218–219 *uentrem…Altissimus*: cf. Ps 45:5.

222–223 *uite auctorem*: cf. Act 3:15.

confessione eructuans uerbum bonum. Corde enim creditur ad iusticiam, ore autem confessio fit ad salutem. Preoccupauit faciem Saluatoris in confessione, pio ausu interrupit sermonem loquentis. Fecitque eum sibi intendere uelut indignata quod sacrum eius eloquium tam copiose stillaret supra ingratos et malos. Ac si diceret: Vsquequo, Domine, seminas in spinis tam male pungentibus ut dicant te in Beelzebub eicere demonia? Vsquequo sanctum das latrantibus et margaritas grunnientibus? Numquid bonum est sumere panem filiorum et mittere canibus non ad manducandum sed ad conculcandum? Intende pocius confessioni mee, quia iam fidem inspirasti ancille tue. Non te permitto diutius loqui ingratis et blasphemis, etiam si dicas michi, 'Dimitte me ut loquar adhuc populo huic,' sicut olim dixisti Moysi famulo tuo, *Dimitte me ut irascatur furor meus contra populum istum dure ceruicis et deleam eos.* Nam nec ipse dimisit te ut deleres populum peccantem, nec ego dimitto te loqui diutius ad populum blasphemantem. Intende pocius michi et exaudi confessionem meam, qua clarius reboante tinniant aures peruersorum et obstruatur os loquentium iniqua. Audi, audi confessionem meam iamiam cum multo deuocionis impetu erumpentem: *Beatus uenter qui te portauit et ubera que suxisti.*

Hac deuotissime mulieris non improba sed fideli et pia exclamatione Dominus delectatus, omisso sermone quem ingerebat ingratis, hilariter ad eam conuertitur, et uerbum eius bonum insigniter approbat, dum quod ab illa minus dictum erat sui annexione sermonis supplere dignatur, *Quin immo*, inquiens, *beati qui audiunt uerbum Dei et custodiunt illud.* Quo nimirum uerbo premissam prudentissime mulieris sentenciam sic approbat ut

227 *eructans uerbum bonum*: cf. Ps 44:2.
227–228 *Corde...salutem*: Rom 10:10.
231–232 *supra...malos*: Lc 6:35.
232 *seminas in spinis*: cf. Mt 13:22 and Mc 4:18.
234 *sanctum...grunnientibus*: cf. Mt 7:6.
235 *bonum...canibus*: cf. Mt 15:26 and Mc 7:27.
240–241 *Dimitte...eos*: cf. Ex 32:9–10.
243–244 *Intende...meam*: cf. Ps 54:3.
251–252 *et...approbat*: cf. Bede, *In Lucam* 4.253 (CCSL 120, p. 237; PL 92:480b).
253–254 *Quin...illud*: Lc 11:28.

etiam temperet; sic temperat ut etiam approbet. Approbat quasi ueram, temperat uero propter auditores ad accusandum et blasphemandum procliues, ne scilicet spiritualium predicator sapere carnem et sanguinem uideretur et suis maternisque laudibus—quod spiritualem non deceret magistrum—mollius deliniri. Itaque ueritati simul et pietati taliter satisfacit, quod superbis et malignis aditum scandali siue calumpnie minime patefacit, illud nobis apostolicum sollicite obseruandum suo prefigens exemplo: *Sermo uester semper in gratia sale sit conditus, ut sciatis quomodo oporteat uos unicuique respondere*. Laudes sibi et matri a pia muliere sollempniter acclamatas propter minus idoneos auditores Dominus sic temperat, ut tamen eisdem matris laudibus subtili responsione multum adiciat, *Quin immo*, / inquiens, et cetera. Quasi diceret: O mulier, magna est fides tua *10r* et preclara confessio tua. Non enim caro et sanguis reuelauit tibi, sed Pater meus qui in celis est, quod beatus uenter qui me portauit, attingentem a fine usque ad finem fortiter. Et beata ubera que suxi, disponens omnia suauiter. Beata plane que me genuit feta de spiritu, aluitque pro tempore, itidem lactescens de spiritu, sed et *beati qui audiunt uerbum Dei et custodiunt illud*, id est factores uerbi et non auditores tantum, in quibus nimirum illa que me genuit et lactauit iure optinet principatum. Tu eam laudas, O mulier, sicut te decet, et ego laudo eam sicut me decet: tu pro eo quod me genuit aluitque uerbum Deum, ego pro eo quod pre cunctis audit et custodit uerbum Dei. Tu pro singulari gratia, ego pro excellenti iusticia. Tu pro eo quod habet incommunicabiliter, ego pro eo quod habet ita cum multis communiter ut tamen pre cunctis habeat excellenter. Tu,

256–260 *Approbat…deliniri*: William suggests that, because it was true, Christ approved of what the woman said, but he tempered her words, lest his detractors think either that he had descended from his discussion of spiritual things into a discussion of fleshly matters, or that he was flattered by the woman's praise.

264–265 *Sermo…respondere*: Col 4:6.

269–270 *O…tua*: Mt 15:28. The passage of imagined speech that follows parallels lines 542–549 in the second half of the homily.

270–271 *Non…est*: Mt 16:17.

272–273 *attingentem…suauiter*: cf. Sap 8:1.

276 *factores…tantum*: Iac 1:22.

282–283 *ego…excellenter*: cf. *Explanatio* 4:6–7 (p. 188).

mulier, in ea laudas uentrem et ubera, ego, Dominus, fidem et opera. Quod tu dicis et quod ego dico iungantur, et perfecta erit laus eius.

Sane quod nemo umquam tam attente audierit, tam sollicite custodierit uerbum Dei quam illa que gignere et alere meruit uerbum Deum, liquido constat neque aliter credi fas est. Quid enim illi deesse poterat in ulla gratia, que omniformis gratie sacris effudit uisceribus effusorem? Quantum, putas, illi gratie spiritualis infudit, quem illa corporaliter mundissime carnis stola indutum ad oculos humanos effudit? Porro quod ille matri tam large infudit, totum illa in filium deuote refudit. Denique nasciturus ex ea Deus preuenit eam in benedictionibus dulcedinis, impertiendo ei quoddam priuilegium gratie, quandam prerogatiuam iusticie, quoddam decus purioris castimonie, quibus prepararetur ad fetum, id est digna foret que, feta non de carne sed de spiritu, Dei filium corporaliter procrearet. Sic ergo sanctificauit eam ad fetum, sed multo uberius, multo insignius, postmodum ex ipso atque in ipso fetu. Si enim futuri fetus gratia, ut diuine dignationi congrueret, singulari excelluit dote uirtutum, quantum illi credimus ex ipso atque in ipso fetu spiritualium accessisse carismatum? Quantum illi credimus influxisse uirtutis et sanctimonie cum Spiritus Sanctus in eam superueniret, uirtus illi Altissimi obumbraret, Dei filius ex eius carne uirginea immaculatum sibi corpus aptaret, corporatum uerbum nouem mensium spacio sacris eius portaretur uisceribus, prolixiori uero tempore sacris eius aleretur uberibus?

284–285 *fidem et opera*: cf. Iac 2:18.

290–294 *Quid…refudit*: William's parallel structure compares the grace that Mary brought into the world by giving birth to Christ with the grace that Christ gave to her when she conceived. Thus *que…effudit* (lines 290–291) refers to Mary giving birth to Christ, while Christ is identified here as *effusorem* (line 291) because he poured (*infudit*) spiritual grace into his mother (*illi quem effudit*).

290 *deesse…gratia*: cf. 1 Cor 1:7.

300-304 *Sic…carismatum*: Mary is sanctified in preparation for conceiving Christ (*ad fetum*), but she is sanctified to a greater degree when she has actually conceived (*ex fetu et in fetu*).

305–306 *Spiritus…obumbraret*: cf. Lc 1:35.

284 ea *LS* : eo *R*

Itaque nemo tam deuote audire, nemo tam perfecte custodire potuit uerbum Dei ut illa que parere meruit uerbum Deum. Et hoc quidem ante partum fecit excellenter futuri partus gratia, sed post partum excellentius, tanta scilicet uirtute quanta / poterat puro homini dari in partu et ex partu accepta. *10v*

Puro inquam homini, nam quod homini in Deum assumpto in ipsa et ex ipsa uerbi unione donatum est modum longissime transcendit humanum. Hoc enim Paulus uocat, *Nomen quod est super omne nomen*, et Iohannes, *Plenitudinem de qua omnes electi accipiunt*, singuli utique pro captu et modulo suo. Erat autem pie uirgini modus quidam largissimus, sed tamen modus utpote homini puro. Cum ergo conciperet et pareret ipsum uas plenitudinis non habentis modum, tantum prioribus eius uirtutibus ex nascentis filii plenitudine adiectum est, quantum capere poterat puri hominis modus. Liquet igitur quia nemo umquam Dominum Saluatorem tam suauiter, tam pie, tam fortiter amauit quam illa que ipsum genuit et lactauit. Amor uero Dei quantus in affectu, tantus et in opere est. Cum enim idem Dominus ait, *Si quis diligit me, sermonem meum seruabit*, ita proculdubio ad amorem sequi obedienciam uoluit, ut amor et obediencia ex equo sibi respondeant, id est tanta sit obediencia quantus amor. Ita ergo si quis diligit eum, sermonem eius seruabit, ut etiam tantum seruet, quantum diligit. Itaque liquet quia nemo umquam sermonem dominicum tantum seruauit, quantum illa que ipsum quam ceteri plus amauit. Illam ergo specialiter respicit, quod Dominus pie mulieri beatum esse uentrem quo portatus fuerat et ubera que suxerat proclamanti respondit, *Quin immo*, inquiens, *beati qui audiunt uerbum Dei*

312–314 *Et…accepta*: cf. *Explanatio* 2:5 and 4:1 (pp 119 and 169).
315–317 *Puro…humanum*: William introduces a discussion of the Virgin's purity by clarifying his previous statement, *quanta poterat puro homini dari* (lines 313–314). The attributive *puro* is elaborated by the predicative *assumpto in Deum in ipsa et ex ipsa unione*; while *quod…donatum est* is the subject of *transcendit*.
317–318 *Nomen…nomen*: Phil 2:9.
318–319 *Plenitudinem…accipiunt*: cf. Io 1:16.
328 *Si…seruabit*: Io 14:23.
337–338 *Quin…illud*: Lc 11:28.

316 uerbi *LS* : etiam ibi *R*

et custodiunt illud. Igitur propter malignantes qui astabant, ne muliebri adulatione palpari uideretur, laudes pie matris sue a muliere dictas sic temperat, ut tamen eisdem multum adiciat, illis quidem ne deteriores blasphemando fierent misericorditer parcens, pios uero auditores subtilius instruens. Ipsi gloria et imperium cum Deo Patre in unitate Spiritus Sancti, Deus per omnia secula seculorum. Amen.

II

⟨H⟩ec de sacra lectione sub paucis uerbis—tam multum acuminis et tam multum dulcedinis occultante—pro nostra tenuitate ad litteram diximus; superest ut, eo donante qui docet hominem scientiam, exinde aliquid morale uel misticum eruamus. Expellit Dominus demonium surdum et mutum; mirantur turbe; malignantur pharisei et scribe, dicentes quod in Beelzebub principe demoniorum eiceret demonia. Quibus respondens Dominus, dum crimen obiectum subtiliter diluit, ad eorum confutandam cecitatem infirmiorem sexum accendit. Nam quedam mulier de turba, dum adhuc loquitur, pre feruore concepte in ipsum deuocionis extollens uocem, id est de pleno pectore pleno etiam gutture uerbum bonum eructuans, *Beatus*, inquit, *uenter qui te portauit et ubera que suxisti*.

Expellit Saluator demonia dum infusione gratie sanat in animis hominum inmissa per inmundos spiritus uicia. Idem quippe inmundi spiritus per uicia que in/mittunt habitationem sibi in *11r* hominibus faciunt. Sane in illa tam feralis, tam insaturabilis odii malignitate quam gratis exercent in homines discreta uidentur

338–342 *Igitur...instruens*: cf. the note on lines 256–260 above. Because of the hostile Scribes and Pharisees (*propter malignantes*, line 338), Christ tempers the woman's words, lest he appear to be flattered by them (*ne...uideretur*, lines 338–339). He stops speaking to the *malignantes* in the crowd (*illis...parcens*, lines 341–342; for a comparable use of *parcere*, see Iob 7:11), for he fears that they will only become worse in their blaspheming (*ne...fierent*, line 341). His words in Lc 11:28 are addressed to the pious members of his audience (*pios...instruens*, line 342).

350–351 *dicentes...demonia*: cf. Lc 11:15.

354 *loquitur*: viz. *Dominus* (lines 351–352).

habere officia. Alius quippe temptat per superbiam et dicitur spiritus superbie, alius per iracundiam et dicitur spiritus iracundie, alius per luxuriam et dicitur spiritus fornicationis, et sic in ceteris. Et hec quidem sollempnia in litteris patrum. Sed et in lege sacra spiritus zelotipie dicitur qui temptat per zelotipiam, stupri scilicet suspicionibus caritatem uulnerans coniugalem. Ille quoque spiritus qui exicialem animo inmittit torporem, ut nec uerba Dei libenter audiat nec gratiarum actioni assuescat, recte dicitur demonium surdum et mutum, ab effectu scilicet quod faciat surdos ad audiendam legem, mutos ad gratiarum actionem.

Sunt autem nonnulli existimantes se nulli demonio subditos, eo quod non occidant, non mechentur, non furentur, nec aliquid graue committant; illo tamen exiciali tepore torpentes, demonium surdum et mutum pati probantur. Porro huius demonii difficilis expulsio, id est inmissi ab hoc inmundo spiritu uicii difficilis curatio est, quia ut ait pater Augustinus, 'Nemo insanabilior est eo qui sibi sanus uidetur;' et hoc subtiliter uerbis euangelicis significatur cum dicitur, *Erat Ihesus eiciens demonium, et illud erat mutum. Erat*, inquit, *eiciens*, id est cum aliqua mora hoc faciens quasi difficultatem patiens, non quod in hoc omnipotens aliquid difficultatis passus fuerit, sed quam egre et difficulter uicium teporis sanetur morula illa significare uoluit.

Super expulsione demonii mirantur turbe, quia et seculares plerumque homines compuncti dant gloriam Deo in conuersione peccatoris, maxime si famosus fuerit. Verum scribe et pharisei hoc inuertunt et calumpniantur, assignantes expulsionem demoniorum Beelzebub principi eorum. Sunt enim in ecclesia quidam mali interpretes operum piorum, ceca malignitate et maligna cecitate inuertentes quicquid pie et honeste fit,

363–365 *Alius...fornicationis*: cf. John Cassian, *De coenobiorum institutis* 6 *spiritus fornicacionis*, 8 *spiritus iracundie*, and 12 *spiritus superbie* (CSEL 17, pp 113–127, 149–165, 204–231; PL 49:265b–292b, 321c–352b, 419b–476b).

367 *spiritus zelotipie*: Num 5:14.

375 *non occidant...furentur*: cf. Ex 20:13–15.

379–380 *Nemo...uidetur*: Augustine, *In Psalmum lviii Ennaratio* 2.8 (CCSL 39, p. 751; PL 36:711).

381–382 *Erat...mutum*: Lc 11:14.

dicentes scilicet illum uel illum non sincere, id est non causa pietatis, illis uel illis uiciis renunciasse, sed pocius causa uanitatis, id est ut ametur, laudetur, honoretur ab hominibus, quibus antea perosus erat propter illa mala. Illum inquam uel illum non causa Dei esse conuersum, sed causa inanis glorie, amore proprie excellencie, qui superbia dicitur. Sicque id quod per spiritum Dei in illo uel illo homine fit, ascribunt Beelzebub principi demoniorum, id est superbie que est caput omnium uiciorum.

His respondet Veritas Sathanan a Sathana non posse expelli, sed in spiritu Dei demonia eici. Sicut enim cognate sunt uirtutes et nulla uirtus aliam inpugnat, ita etiam cognata sunt uicia, nec ullum uicium aliud effugat. Sed nimirum sicut una plerumque uirtus intermittitur dum ab alia uirtute mens fortius rapitur, ita etiam unum plerumque uicium, dum aliud fortius allicit, intermitti—non dimitti—contingit. Quippe aliud est intermittere, aliud dimittere, nec dimittit qui intermittit. Nam quod actu intermittitur, affectu retinetur. Sic ergo Sathanas plerumque Sathane cedit, / numquam autem Sathanas Sathanan eicit. *11v*

Disserente autem Veritate contra blasphemos, et precedentis signi potenciam et salubris uerbi sapientiam admirans pariter et uenerans quedam mulier de turba non summisse sed tanto sollempnius quanto et deuocius extollens uocem, *Beatus*, inquit, *uenter qui te portauit et ubera que suxisti*. Sane hanc mulierem siue ecclesie catholice siue pie cuiuslibet anime tipum gessisse dicamus, conueniens et ratum est. Nam quod pia quelibet anima facit, ecclesia facit, cum nichil sit ecclesia nisi piarum unitas animarum. Fecit Saluator mira, dixit salubria,

401 *id…uiciorum*: cf. Augustine, *De civitate Dei* 14.3.2 (CCSL 48, p. 417, PL 41:406).

402 *Sathanan*: a Greek accusative.

403 *cognate sunt uirtutes*: Bede, *Allegorica expositio in Parabolas Salomonis* 1.2 (CCSL 119b, p. 35; PL 91:946d).

407–408 *ita…contingit*: an accusative-infinitive construction, with *unum uicium* as the subject of the infinitives *intermitti* and *non dimitti*.

416–418 *Sane…est*: cf. Bede, *In Lucam* 4.241–244 (CCSL 120, p. 237, PL 92:480a–b).

420–424 *Fecit…uerbis*: a justification for the typological or allegorical reading of the biblical text. William states that Christ's actions are as meaningful as his words, and that Christ intended them to be understood in that way. For discussions of such theories of allegory,

et quandoque sermonem confirmauit sequentibus signis, quandoque etiam signa que infamabantur a perfidis purgauit sequentibus uerbis, manifeste insinuans in opere sancte predicationis uicissim indigere et uerba signis et signa uerbis. Miratur et ueneratur ecclesia, seu pia et fidelis anima, proprii Saluatoris et potenciam in signis et sapientiam in uerbis, et e conuerso sapientiam in signis, potenciam in uerbis. Verbo siquidem eiciebat demonia, uerbo curabat infirmitates. Vnde centurio, *Tantum*, inquit, *dic uerbo, et sanabitur puer meus*. Itaque uerbo eius quid fortius? Sed et in signis corporalibus nichil fecit quo non aliquid spirituale misticumque signaret, eratque non tantum in uerbis sed et in signis eius celestis doctrine uigor. Et potentiam quidem eius, siue in signis siue in uerbis, quia inpromptu est, non oportet rimari sed mirari et deuote uenerari. Porro quia scriptum est, *Trahitur sapientia de occultis*, eius siue in signis siue in uerbis sapientiam primum oportet studiose rimari, dehinc pie mirari et deuote uenerari. Cui autem non datur eam acute rimari, sufficit latentem pie uenerari. Ergo siue pro sui sensus acumine sufficiat siue pro sua simplicitate non sufficiat sapientiam trahere de occultis, id est scripture sacre misteria penetrare, nichilominus fidelis anima pro studio pietatis et feruore deuocionis in laudibus Saluatoris uocem exaltat; beatum uentrem qui eum portauit et ubera que sugere dignatus est sollempni acclamatione pronunciat.

Quippe cum per consideratam signorum eius potentiam seu uerborum eius sapientiam ad acclamandas ei laudes accenditur, familiarius atque suauius se menti contuendam prebet dignatio

---

see Denys Turner, *Eros and Allegory: Medieval Exegesis of the Song of Songs* (Kalamazoo, Mich., 1995); *idem*, "Allegory in Christian Late Antiquity," in *The Cambridge Companion to Allegory*, ed. R. Copeland and P. Struck (Cambridge, forthcoming).

424 *uicissim...uerbis*: an accusative-infinitive construction following *insinuans*: *uerba* and *signa* are the accusative subjects of *indigere*, while *signis* and *uerbis* are its ablative objects.

428–429 *Tantum...meus*: Mt 8:8, cf. Lc 7:7.

433 *inpromptu*: 'apparent.'

435 *Trahitur...occultis*: Iob 28:18.

445–448 *Quippe...maiestas*: supply *anima* from line 441 as the subject of *accenditur*; *eius* and *ei* likewise refer to *Saluatoris* in line 442. The subject of *prebet* is *dignatio*, which shows itself to the mind

quam maiestas. Denique oculo mentis intendere in maiestatem sic est ac si oculo carnis intendas in solem. Vnde scriptum est, *Sicut qui mel comedit multum non est ei bonum, sic qui scrutator est maiestatis opprimetur a gloria*. Proinde mens pia et cauta parce et pauide, atque ideo parce quia pauide, intendit in maiestatem; porro dignationem, que non est aliud quam spontanea inclinatio maiestatis, hilaribus atque irreuerberatis oculis contuetur. *Magnus Dominus et magna uirtus eius, et sapientie eius non est numerus*: hoc maiestatis est. *Paruulus natus est nobis, filius datus est nobis, et factus est principatus super humerum eius*: hoc dignationis est. Illud habet plus timoris et terroris, hoc uero plus suauitatis et amoris. Vtrumque dixit Propheta, scilicet, *Timete Dominum omnes sancti eius*, et, *Diligite Dominum omnes sancti eius*. Illud respectu maiestatis, hoc uero respectu dig/nationis. Nam respectus maiestatis *12r*
propensius incitat timorem, respectus uero dignationis uehementius excitat amorem. Item ait, *Seruite Domino in timore*:

---

for contemplation more familiarly and more sweetly than majesty. William is describing a devotional or mystical progression in the soul, beginning with it being incited to the praise of God, then moving to contemplation of the divine *dignatio*, and finally to contemplation of the divine *maiestas*, the last very rarely and only ever intermittently achieved. This movement is reminiscent of William's discussion of the liturgy raising the soul up to be like the angels in the *Sermo de Trinitate*, esp. lines 570–571. *Dignatio* is a term with rich theological significance, referring especially to God's self-abasement for the sake of humanity in the Incarnation. With this in mind, it might best be translated 'love' or 'mercy.' William glosses it as *non aliud quam spontanea inclinatio maiestatis* (line 453–454).

448–449 *Denique…solem*: cf., inter alia, Augustine, *Soliloquia* 1.6 (CSEL 89, pp 19–22; PL 32:875–876).

450–451 *Sicut…gloria*: Prov 25:27.

451–455 *Proinde…contuetur*: as noted above, William writes that the mind is only able to contemplate the divine majesty for very brief periods of time, but here he notes that the relationship that the mind discerns between divine mercy and majesty makes the contemplation of mercy all the more pleasing.

455–456 *Magnus…numerus*: Ps 146:5.

456–458 *Paruulus…eius*: Is 9:6.

460 *Timite…eius*: Ps 33:10.

461 *Diligite…eius*: Ps 30:24.

464 *Seruite…timore*: Ps 2:11.

hoc debetur maiestati. Dignationi quid? Certe quod alibi ait: *Seruite Domino in leticia*, id est in suauitate amoris.

Si enim timendus quia excelsus et magnus, nonne amandus quia propter nos humilis et paruulus? Nam dum esset in forma Dei, exinaniuit semetipsum, formam serui accipiens. Denique ipsa Veritas: *Nolite*, inquit, *timere eos qui occidunt corpus, animam autem non possunt occidere*, hoc est nolite timere homines. Quid ergo? *Sed eum*, inquit, *timete qui habet potestatem et animam et corpus perdere in gehenna*, hoc est timete maiestatem. Si autem timendus qui habet potestatem perdere in gehenna, nonne amandus qui liberat a gehenna? Sicut ergo maiestas timorem, ita etiam dignatio exigit amorem. Vterque uero, id est siue timor siue amor, mixtum habet stuporem. Stupet enim timor, stupet et amor. Stupet timor ad incomprehensibilitatem maiestatis, stupet et amor ad magnitudinem dignationis. Quia igitur timor habet aculeos, amor uero delicias, iccirco familiarius est anime pie intendere in dignationem quam in maiestatem, hoc est in inclinationem quam in apicem maiestatis. Huc accedit quod apex maiestatis tam longe est supra nos, inclinatio uero eius est usque ad nos, secundum illud Apostoli: *In similitudinem hominum factus, et habitu inuentus ut homo.* Nec mirum si laboret mens pia intendere in id quod tam longe supra se est, familiare uero habeat intendere in id quod sibi tam uicine approximat. Proinde significata per deuotissimam illam mulierem fidelis anima, signis pariter et uerbis redemptoris excitata atque edocta, dignationi potius quam maiestati laudes acclamat, *Beatus*, inquiens, *uenter qui te portauit et ubera que suxisti.*

Quante enim dignationis est, quod ille qui portat omnia uerbo uirtutis sue, utero propter nos uoluit portari femineo, ille itidem qui implet omne animal benedictione, lacte propter nos uoluit pasci femineo. Verumptamen in tanta dignatione eius nequaquam peregrinata seu periclitata est dignitas. Nempe quoad licuit sine periculo dignitatis extendit dignationem. Ser-

466 *Seruite…leticia*: Ps 99:2.
468–469 *esset…accipiens*: cf. Phil 2:6–7.
470–471 *Nolite…occidere*: Mt 10:28.
472–473 *Sed…gehenna*: cf. Mt 10:28.
485 *In…homo*: Phil 2:7.

uauit decus maiestatis inclinando maiestatem ad opus pietatis. Inclinauit enim maiestatem, non fedauit. Itaque utero propter nos uoluit portari femineo sed uirgineo, et lac propter nos uoluit sugere femineum sed uirgineum. Hic posuit metas dignationis. Hucusque licuit sine lesione dignitatis. Dominum glorie uterus non dedecuit femineus quia uirgineus siue lac femineum quia uirgineum. Non horruit uterum uel ubera uirginis amator puritatis. Porro uiscera uberaque non uirginea decus exhorruit maiestatis. Sane Dominus glorie in illo sublimi incarnationis sue misterio pro sua dignitate exhorruit semen uirile et uterum defloratum siue etiam deflorandum: semen uirile, / ne *12v* in feditate concupiscencie Dominus glorie conciperetur; uterum defloratum seu deflorandum, ne uel ab ea conciperetur quam aliquando concupiscencia maculasset seu maculatura esset.

Itaque pro dignitate nascituri parum fuit in sacro illo conceptu concupiscenciam non esse; nam dignitatis ratio plus exigebat in illa scilicet que Dominum glorie concipiebat concupiscenciam numquam fuisse uel fore. Non potuit Dei filius ad opus salutis nostre ueniens esse filius uiri sed nec femine uel antea deflorate uel postea deflorande. Plane non potuit, quia ipsum non decuit. Nam hoc solum laudabiliter non potest omnipotens, quod ipsum non decet. Porro non dedecuit amatorem puritatis esse filium perpetue uirginis. Itaque et pro sua dignitate potuit et pro ratione salutis nostre uoluit esse filius uirginis. Non potuit se pro nobis Dei filius humilius inclinare quam ut fieret filius femine, seruata nimirum inuiolabili dignitate sua, qua scilicet non poterat esse filius tunc uel antea deflorate seu postea deflorande. Inclinauit ergo se pro nobis quoad licuit, id est quoad decuit extendit dignationem usque ad ultimos, ut ita dicam, fines dignitatis.

Huic tante tam preclare, tam stupende dignationi diuine pia quelibet anima quanta potest uocis et mentis sollempnitate applaudit, *Beatus*, inquiens, *uenter qui te portauit et ubera que suxisti*. Quod utique facit quando iuxta propheticam admoni-

503–512 *Dominum*...*esset*: cf. *Explanatio* 7:1–2 (pp 304–306).

513–516 *Itaque*...*fore*: this sentence contains two separate accusative-infinitive constructions: the first as the subject of *fuit*, the second as the object of *exigebat*.

tionem seruit Domino non tantum in timore, respectu scilicet maiestatis, sed etiam in leticia, respectu scilicet dignationis. Quantoque seruit Domino sincerius atque deuocius, tanto in eius laudem uocem extollit fortius et altius. Tantum clamat, quantum amat. Nempe tantus est pie mentis clamor ad Deum, quantus et amor in Deum. Immo eius clamor non nisi amor est, eius clamare non nisi amare est. Et quid respondet Dominus? Neque enim silet ad pie mentis clamorem. *Quin immo*, inquit, *beati qui audiunt uerbum Dei et custodiunt illud*. Quasi diceret: Bene facis applaudens preclare dignationi mee, sed et ego congratulor huic tam pure et tam feruide deuotioni tue. Tu beatum dicis uentrem qui me corporaliter portauit Dominum glorie et ubera que me corporaliter aluerunt caput ecclesie, sed et ego beata dico uiscera que michi spiritualiter parturiunt et ubera que michi spiritualiter nutriunt filios adoptionis. Tu beatificas matrem carnis mee Mariam, sed et ego beatifico matrem menbrorum meorum ecclesiam. Quid enim est ecclesia nisi illi qui audiunt uerbum Dei et custodiunt illud?

Matrem capitis mater menbrorum preclare imitatur in uirginitate simul et fecunditate. Vtraque enim uirgo: illa in carne, hec in fide. Vtraque grauida de Spiritu Sancto: illa ut corporaliter pareret caput, hec ut spiritualiter pariat menbra. Quippe ex eodem spiritu ille natus, nos renati. Et hoc est quod Iohannes ait de filiis adoptionis: *Qui non ex sanguinibus, neque ex uoluntate carnis, neque ex uoluntate uiri, sed ex Deo nati sunt*. Denique in Paulo Apostolo uox grauide ecclesie est:

533–534 *seruit... letitia*: cf. Pss. 2:11 and 99:2; cf. lines 464–466 above.

540–541 *Quin... illud*: Lc 11:28.

542–549 *Bene... ecclesiam*: cf. the similar section in the first half of the homily, lines 269–286 above.

543–549 *Tu... ecclesiam*: cf. *Explanatio* 4:13–14 (p. 205). William imagines Christ identifying himself as the head of the Church (*caput ecclesie*, lines 545, 551, and 554) and faithful Christians as the limbs or members (lines 549, 551, and 554) grafted (*filios adoptionis*, lines 547, 556, and 564) to the body of Christ. Envisioning the Church as Christ's body in such terms was a common motif in medieval literature; Gilbert of Poitiers, for example, identifies the subject matter of the Psalter as 'Christus integer, caput cum membris,' in A. Pagliari, "Il presunto commento cui salmi di S. Lorenzo Giustiani opera di Gilberto porretano," *Ævum* 36 (1962) 423.

556–558 *Qui... sunt*: Io 1:13.

Filioli mei quos iterum parturio donec formetur Christus in uobis. Sed et lactantis ecclesie in eodem uox est: / *Tanquam* 13r *paruulis in Christo lac uobis potum dedi, non escam*. Itaque in apostolico pectore non tantum ecclesie uiscera sed etiam ubera fuere, uiscera scilicet quibus parturiret et ubera quibus enutriret sponso celesti filios adoptionis.

Scriptum est de Adam quod genuerit ad imaginem et similitudinem suam filium quem uocauit Seth. Audi et Paulum, immo in Paulo ecclesiam spiritualiter gignentem ad imaginem et similitudinem suam filios: *Imitatores*, inquit, *mei estote, sicut et ego Christi*. Idem quoque loquens ad regem Agrippam, expressit in semetipso formam ecclesie in fetum numerosiorem gestientis atque ad imaginem et similitudinem suam gignere cupientis. *Opto*, inquit, *apud Deum et in modico et in magno, non tantum te sed et omnes qui audiunt tales fieri qualis sum ego, exceptis uinculis his*. Porro cum quanto dolore et difficultate filios ecclesie parturiret aperit ipse dicens, *Quis infirmatur et ego non infirmor? Quis scandalizatur et ego non uror?* Et alibi: *Supra modum*, inquit, *grauati sumus, supra uirtutem ita ut tederet nos etiam uiuere*. Itaque impletum est in eius materno pectore illud dominicum: *Mulier cum parit tristiciam habet*. Sed et illud quod sequitur, in eo consequenter implebatur: *Cum autem pepererit puerum, iam non meminit pressure propter gaudium*. Audi gloriantem in filiis, audi immemorem pressure propter gaudium. Tessalonicensibus quos utique Deo genuerat, quos cum multo labore parturierat, sicut ipse dicit, *Nocte et die laborantes, ne quem uestrum grauaremus predicauimus uobis euangelium*, ita scribit, *Que est nostra spes aut gaudium aut corona glorie? Nonne uos ante Dominum nostrum Ihesum Christum in aduentu eius?*

559–560 *Filioli…uobis*: Gal. 4:19.
560–561 *Tanquam…escam*: 1 Cor 3:1–2.
565–566 *genuerit…Seth*: cf. Gen 5:3.
568–569 *Imitatores…Christi*: 1 Cor 11:1.
572–574 *Opto…his*: Act 26:29.
575–576 *Quis…uror*: 2 Cor 11:29.
577–578 *Supra…uiuere*: 2 Cor 1:8.
579-582 *Mulier…gaudium*: cf. Io 16:21.
585–586 *Nocte…euangelium*: 1 Thess 2:9.
586–588 *Que…eius*: 1 Thess 2:19.

Studeamus et nos, carissimi, pro modulo nostro prolem Deo gignere, uitantes sollicite maledictum sterilitatis. Maledictus enim qui non fecerit semen in Israel. Cui nimirum maledicto supponitur qui neminem Deo lucratur uel saltem lucrari conatur. Nam quantum in se est lucratur, qui lucrari conatur, iuxta illud: *Si ibi fuerit filius pacis, requiescet super eum pax uestra, sin autem, ad uos reuertetur*. Si datus est tibi sermo sapientie siue sermo scientie, non abscondas pecuniam Domini tui in terra, sed expende ad lucrum et lucrare Deo quos potes, semine uerbi gignens ei filios, ita nimirum ut quod plantas uerbo riges exemplo. Si autem minus potes uerbo, esto proximo ad bene uiuendum uel exemplar, iuxta illud: *Videant opera uestra bona et glorificent Patrem uestrum qui in celis est*. Quod si nec exemplo uales, siue propter secretiorem conuersationem, siue propter infirmitatem occultiorem, siue quia falsiloquis famam tuam lacerantibus non bene de te sentiunt homines, orationi inuigila et orando fac lucrum de proximis, memor illius uerbi apostolici: *Multum enim ualet deprecatio iusti assidua*. Porro si neque uerbo, neque exemplo, neque orationis studio quemquam Deo lucrifacis, time illud: *Vtinam calidus esses aut frigidus, sed quia tepidus es, incipiam te euomere / ex ore meo*. Quippe per *13v*
tepidum sterilis quisque a fructu bonorum operum designatur, cui nimirum satis est illius prophetice exhortationis, *Declina a malo et fac bonum*, dimidium obseruare, scilicet, *Declina a malo*. Non occidit, non mechatur, non furatur, non concupiscit

590–591 *Maledictus…Israel*: cf. Jerome, *Adversus Jovinianum* 1.22 (PL 23:241b); cf. Deut 7:14 (Vetus Latina), Ex 23:26. This adaptation of the biblical text was a common motif throughout literature of the twelfth century: see Rachel Fulton, *From Judgment to Passion*, p. 590 n. 129.

591–592 *Cui…conatur*: *qui neminem Deo lucratur uel saltem lucrari conatur* is the subject of *supponitur* ('he…is added to' or 'he…is counted among'), with *cui maledicto* as the indirect object of the main verb.

594–595 *Si…reuertetur*: Lc 10:6.

596–597 *non…terra*: cf. Mt 25:18.

600–601 *Videant…est*: Mt 5:16.

606 *Multum…assidua*: Iac 5:16.

608–609 *Vtinam…meo*: Apoc 3:15–16.

611–612 *Declina…bonum*: Ps 36:27.

613–614 *Non…sui*: cf. Ex 20:13–15 and 17.

rem proximi sui, animo et actu tenet innocenciam, sed sine beneficiencia. Declinans a malo et non faciens bonum, inter bonum et malum quodam, ut ita dicam, meditullio est contentus. Ita neque faciendo malum frigidus, neque bonum faciendo calidus, sed neutrum faciendo inter frigidum et calidum medius, id est tepidus, inuenitur. Sane innocencia sine beneficiencia parum ualet et quasi nauseam Deo prouocat dum non placet. *Quia*, inquit, *tepidus es, incipiam te euomere ex ore meo.*

Ergo quicumque uis fructum facere in Israel, ne incurras maledictum sterilitatis, tene innocenciam cum beneficiencia, a malo declinare non contentus, ad bona facienda accingere, et iuxta Salomonem, *Quodcumque potest manus tua facere, instanter operare*, ut quantum in te est aliquos Deo lucreris, quia ut ait Gregorius, 'Nullum Deo tale sacrificium quale zelus animarum.' Habe uiscera caritatis quibus parturias, cum uberibus pietatis quibus enutrias, quantum in te est, filios Deo, ut et in te redundet preclara illa benedictio mirabilis femine: *Beatus uenter qui te portauit et ubera que suxisti.* Nempe cum aliquos Christo lucrifacis, Christum in illis concipis et parturis et paris et nutris, iuxta quod ipse ait: *Quod uni ex minimis meis fecistis, michi fecistis.* Ipsi gloria, laus, et imperium, in secula seculorum. Amen.

621 *Quia...meo*: Apoc 3:16.
622 *facere in Israel*: cf. Jerome, *Adversus Jovinianum* 1.22 (PL 23:241b); cf. Deut 7:14 (Vetus Latina), Ex 23:26.
625–626 *Quodcumque...operare*: Eccl 9:10.
627–628 *Nullum...animarum*: Gregory the Great, *Homiliarum in Ezechielem Prophetam* 12.30 (CCSL 142, pp 200–201; PL 76:932c).
633–634 *Quod...fecistis*: cf. Mt 25:40.

622 fructum *LS* : sanctum *R*

III Sermo de Sancto Albano

Edited from
London, Lambeth Palace Library, MS 73, fols 115vb–121ra

SERMO DE SANCTO ALBANO

Inter rosas martyrum rutilat insigniter noster Albanus. 115vb Confidenter dico nostrum, calumpnias Britonum non formidans. 'Quid uobis,' inquiunt, 'et Brithoni Albano? Angli estis. Patres uestri gentem eius exterminauerunt. Locum eius cum corpore occupauerunt, et uos in peccato patrum uestrorum perseueratis usque ad diem hanc. An ideo uestrum dicitis, quia captiuum tenetis?' Immo nobis Anglis et eggregio martiri multum per omnem modum. Quid autem illi et uobis, O Britones? Offensus peccatis gentis sue, que iam usque ad celum peruenerant, transiuit ad Anglos, atque, ut ita dicam, ex Britone Anglus, ex uestro noster factus est. Quod si inde gloriandum putatis quia uester secundum carnem, hanc gloriationem inanem ostendit qui ait, *Caro non prodest quicquam*. Ergo, ut dixi, inter rosas martyrum insi⟨g⟩niter rutilat noster Albanus.

Sed numquid rubet inter rosas et non candet inter lilia? Loquitur sponsa in Canticis de summo martyre, martyrum capite, *Dilectus*, inquiens, *meus candidus et rubicundus*. Quale autem capud, talia et membra. In tantum enim membra, in quantum similitudo capitis in eis. Vnde et propheta, cum sancta quatuor animalia describeret, *Similitudo*, inquid, *hominis in eis*. Cuius hominis? Certe illius de quo Apostolus, *Secundus*, inquid, *homo de celo celestis*. Et addit, *Quale celestis, tales et celestes*. Ergo

4 *Quid...Albano*: 'What do you have to do with the Briton Alban?' cf. lines 8–9 below.
6–7 *uos...hanc*: cf. Esdr 9:7.
8–9 *Immo...modum*: see the note on line 4 above.
9–10 *Offensus...peruenerant*: cf. Apoc 18:5.
14 *Caro...quicquam*: Io 6:64.
17 *de...capite*: i.e. Christ.
18 *Dilectus...rubicundus*: Cant 5:10.
21 *Similitudo...eis*: Ez 1:5.
22–23 *Secundus...celestes*: 1 Cor 15:47–48. As in the sermon on Luc 11:27 (lines 543–549), here William compares Christ as the head of the Church to the body of faithful Christians, in this case referring specifically to the martyrs.

1 SERMO...ALBANO *supplied from a list of contents on fol. 2v S : omitted by L, which here reads* Item tractatus eiusdem ad eundem de Sancto Albano **2–173** Inter...quem *a quire, as noted above (p. 24), is missing here in S*

quale capud martyrum, tales et martyres. Ergo et ipsi non tantum rubicundi sed eciam candidi, distincte tamen. Quippe illi ideo candidi, quia candidati; ille uero ita candidus, quod non candidatus. Ille inquam candidus natus, et ideo minime candidatus; illi uero tetri nati, sed renascendo candidati. Quia ergo similitudo / hominis in eis, illius inquam hominis de quo dicitur, *116ra* *Dilectus meus candidus et rubicundus*, eciam ipsi sunt candidi et rubicundi. In uita candidi, in morte rubicundi. Candidi remissione peccatorum et mundicia morum, rubicundi uero cruore martyrii. Plus dico: ipsa morte in conspectu Domini pretiosa, non tantum rubicundi, sed eciam candidi, et tanto candidiores, quanto rubicundiores. Nichil enim sic ad purum emundat, nichil sic dealbat, ut sanguis martyrii. Inde est quod Iohannes in Apocalipsi martyres uidit stolis albis amictos et audiuit de eis, *Hii sunt qui uenerunt ex magna tribulatione, et lauerunt stolas suas, et dealbauerunt eas in sanguine agni*. Cum enim dealbantur in sanguine suo, non nisi in sanguine agni dealbantur, per quem scilicet sanguis eorum sacer est. Nam sanguis summi martyris imitatorum suorum sanguinem consecrauit. Inter hos sane noster Albanus amictus est stola alba, et ideo uere 'Albanus.' Dealbauit eum sanguis agni, dealbauit eum sanguis

25–28 *Quippe…candidati*: William distinguishes between Christ, who was *candidus* from birth, from the martyrs, such as Alban, who had to become *candidus*, i.e. who were *candidatus*.

29 *similitudo…eis*: Ez 1:5.

30 *Dilectus…rubicundus*: Cant 5:10.

31 *In…rubicundi*. cf. Jerome, *Commentariorum in Esaiam* 14.53.1 and 17.63.1 (CCSL 73A, pp 589 and 721; PL 24:506 and 610); *idem*, *Adversus Jovinianum* 1.31 (PL 23:254b). All of William's writing on this theme is based on the Hieronymic interpretation of Cant 5:10. This motif was popular in medieval commentaries on the Canticle of Canticles, such as those by Bede (PL 91:116a) and Haimo of Auxerre (PL 70:1085; attributed there to Cassiodorus), though no other writer appears to have developed it as fully as William; cf. *Explanatio* 5.10 (pp 249–250).

33 *ipsa…pretiosa*: cf. Ps 115:15.

37–39 *Hii…agni*: cf. Apoc 7:14.

43–44 *amictus…agni*: cf. Apoc 7:13–14. William also describes Mary dressed in a 'stolam candidam, stolam immortalitatis,' and his description of Alban here is reminiscent of his account of Mary. *Explanatio* 2:10–13 (p. 131).

proprius, et ideo uere 'Albanus.' Olim quidem nomine, nunc autem re 'Albanus.'

Et forte nemo erat in cognatione eius qui uocaretur hoc nomine, sed, uelud quodam presagio futuri, inditum est ei hoc nomen. Nam preordinati ad stolam albam aptum nomen 'Albanus.' Homines illi tale nomen dederunt; Deus autem, ut hoc nomen esset aptum illi, aptauit eum nomini, largiendo graciam qua dealbaretur in sanguine agni. Homo, inquam, dedit illi nomen, Deus rem nominis. Homo eum dixit, Deus autem fecit 'Albanum.' Fecit eum Deus non tantum rubicundum sed eciam candidum, non tantum rosam / sed eciam lilium, atque *116rb* ideo uere 'Albanum.'

Erant plane beati martyres non tantum rose sed eciam lilia; foris rose, intus lilia; ad homines rose, ad Deum lilia; quantum rose, tantum lilia. Nam pro modo ruboris erat in eis et modus candoris. Quantum foris passione rubebant, tantum intus luce puritatis candebant. Illud ergo sponse in Canticis, *Dilectus meus michi et ego illi, qui pascitur inter lilia*, prerogatiue martirum aptissime conuenit. Pascitur inter lilia lilium liliorum; pascit secum martyres summus martyr, capud martyrum. Ipse enim pascit et ipse pascitur. Pascit in eo quod Deus; pascitur in eo quod homo. Sed non solus pascitur, pascit enim suos secum: illos precipue qui dealbauerunt stolas suas in sanguine eius, digni plane appellari lilia et pasci in eternis deliciis cum lilio liliorum.

Et notandum quod sponsus qui est et rosa et lilium—rosa propter ruborem passionis, lilium propter singularis candorem puritatis, ac per hoc rosa rosarum, sicut et lilium liliorum—non dicitur 'inter rosas,' sed 'inter lilia.' Et quidem martires, ut superius ostendimus, ex ipsa passione non tantum rubicundi sed eciam candidi extitere. Quantum enim rubuere foris, tantum ex ipso rubore ad candorem creuere intus. Ex ipsa ergo passione non tantum rose sed eciam lilia fuere. At non ita summus martyr, capud et Dominus martyrum. Non enim canduit ex passione, non per ruborem creuit ad candorem, ut ceteri. De

47 *cognatione*: 'family, blood relations.'
52 *dealbaretur... agni*: cf. Apoc 7:14.
61–62 *Dilectus... lilia*: Cant 2:16.
67 *dealbauerunt... eius*: Apoc 7:14.

Spiritu Sancto conceptus ex uirgine, perfecta et singulari canduit puritate. Itaque rosa fuit ex passione, lilium uero ex singulari illa conceptione. Prius ergo lilium, / *116va* postea rosa; prius candidus, postea eciam rubicundus, si attendas candorem puritatis quem accepit ex conceptione. Nam si attendis in eo candorem inmortalitatis, quem accepit ex resurrectione, prius rosa, postea lilium; prius rubicundus, postea candidus. Ex passione tantum rosa fuit; ante passionem uero ex singulari conceptione lilium puritatis, post passionem ex gloria resurrectione lilium inmortalitatis. Verum ex conceptione ita est candidus, quod non candidatus. Nam candidus natus: nichil macule nascendo contraxit. Porro ex resurrectione ita est candidus quod eciam candidatus, id est candidus ex atro factus, ex mortali scilicet inmortalis.

Ille candidus nascendo, sui uero candidi renascendo. Verum ille nascendo adeo candidus quod eciam lilium et lilium liliorum; illi uero ita renascendo candidi quod non statim lilia. Nam etsi renascendo nigredine exuuntur, non tamen perfecto statim induuntur. Denique paulatim usque ad eximium candorem proficiunt, et sic lilia fiunt. Verum hoc paucorum est. Martyres uero, etsi ante passionem lilia non erant, in ipsa et ex ipsa passione lilia fiunt. Etsi qui ante passionem hoc erant, in ipsa et ex ipsa passione hoc illustrius fiunt. Et prius quidem fiunt lilia sanctitatis, consequenter futuri lilia eterne iocunditatis. Eo ipso quo rose fiunt uel insignius fiunt lilia sanctitatis, porro ex rosis fiunt lilia iocunditatis. Hic ergo sunt rose simul et lilia, in eterna beatitudine non rose, sed ex rosis lilia, de quibus dicitur, *Dilectus meus michi et ego illi, qui pascitur inter lilia.* Lilium liliorum pascitur inter lilia, pascendo secum lilia. Pascit, inquam, secum lilium / *116vb* sanctitatis, ea secum pascendo efficiens lilia iocunditatis.

Hic quidem martyres sunt rose, ubi scilicet habundant spine. Vbi uero non sunt spine persecutionis nec rose passionis. Hic rose, ibi ex rosis lilia; et propterea lilium liliorum non dicitur pasci 'inter rosas,' sed 'inter lilia.' Ibi plane noster Albanus, utpote candidissimum iuxta proprietatem sui nominis ex rubentissima rosa lilium, pascitur cum lilio liliorum; quantum hic olim uel ex perfecta uite mundicia uel ex sacratissima passione lilium sanctitatis, tantum, immo multo amplius cum summo martyre, martyrum capite, lilium iocunditatis. Nam ut ait Apos-

tolus, *Non sunt condigne passiones huius temporis ad futuram gloriam, que reuelabitur in nobis*. Et quidem pro mensura meriti erit et mensura premii, iuxta illud: *In qua mensura mensi fueritis, remecietur uobis*. Sed tamen pius remunerator secundum diuicias gracie sue plurimum supererogabit. Vnde idem Dominus, cum dixisset, *In qua mensura mensi fueritis, remecietur uobis*, contextum annexuit, *et adicietur uobis*.

Age nunc, iuxta ueracis Bede historiam, qualiter et quantum idem athleta noster suo per superni prouisoris graciam aptatus sit nomini uideamus. Certe omnes concupiscencialiter descendentes ex Adam atri nascuntur, quia filii ire et ob hoc eciam filii gehenne nascuntur. Siue ex atris siue ex albis, id est siue ex peccatoribus siue ex iustis nascantur, nonnisi atri, id est peccatores, nascuntur. Siue ex coruis siue ex columbis nascantur, nonnisi corui nascuntur. Sane noster Albanus peccator ex peccatoribus, ater ex atris, coruus ex coruis natus est, et tamen idem corui natum ex se coruum 'Albanum ' uocauerunt. / Mira *117ra* quidem sua clemencia, sed mira Dei prouidencia, qui nimirum cuius uult miseretur, et ex atro album et ex coruo cignum facit. Creuit puer nudo adhuc nomine 'Albanus,' immo non nudo nomine sed diuina eciam preordinatione. Nondum inquam re, nec tamen nudo nomine, quia diuina preordinatione 'Albanus.' Adhesit parentibus, didicit opera eorum et seruiuit scultilibus eorum, utpote uere filius coruorum. Et qui erat niger nascendo, factus nigerrimus tenebrarum principibus seruiendo.

Verum ubi habundauit peccatum, superhabundauit et gracia. Preuenit eum superna pietas in benedictionibus dulcedinis,

119–120 *Non...nobis*: Rom 8:18.
121–122 *In...uobis*: Mc 4:24; cf. Mt 7:2, Lc 6:38.
124–125 *In...adicietur uobis*: Mc 4:24; cf. Mt 7:2, Lc 6:38.
126 *iuxta...historiam*: cf. Bede, *Historia* 1.7 (pp 28–35). For a discussion of William's use of Bede's text and a summary of Bede's account of the martyrdom of Alban, see the Introduction, p. 19.
129 *filii ire*: Eph 2:3.
132–133 *Siue...nascuntur*: cf. Cant 5:11–12.
137 *cuius... miseretur*: Rom 9:18.
141–142 *didicit...eorum*: cf. Ps 105:35b–36a.
141 *scultilibus*: 'engraved or sculpted things, idols.'

⇒ **124–125** remecietur : remicietur *L*

quesiuit non querentem se. Feruebant feralia principum edicta contra pios. Fugiebat clericus Christianus rabiem persecutionis; diuertit ad Albanum. Sed paganos fugiens cur diuertit ad paganum? Fugiebat lux tenebras, agnus lupos; et quomodo lux tenebris, agnus lupo se credidit? Nimirum, ut reor, homo Dei responsum acceperat a Spiritu Sancto: 'Vade in Verolamium, precepi enim ibi Albano ut pascat et abscondat te, uerbo uite pascendus et luce ueritatis illustrandus a te.' Suscepit Albanus hospitem per quem dealbaretur, id est suo nomini aptaretur. Misertus est homo hominem, homo homini exibuit humanitatem, et hoc quidem nature debebat. Tenuit legem nature, diuine adhuc expers iusticie. Suscepit enim hominem in nomine hominis; suscepit iustum, sed in nomine iusti. Nondum ergo dignus erat mercede iusti, sed tamen sic preparabatur ad eam, sic approximabat ei. Suscepit Christianum, nondum quidem propter Christum, sed tamen, quia missus erat a Christo, suscepit in Christiano Christum. Ait enim Christus, *Qui accipit si quem misero, me ac/cipit.* *117rb*

Quippe excepit eum in domum suam, sed nondum in cor suum. Tenuit eum, nec dimisit donec introduxit eum in domum cordis sui et in cubiculum mentis sue, secundum illud Apostoli: *Habitare Christum per fidem in cordibus uestris.* Non enim metu impiorum principum pium dimisit hospitem, in quo Christum susceperat, sed tutas ei pro tempore latebras procurabat. Pascebat eum et pascebatur ab eo. Abscondebat eum a facie tempestatis et illustrabatur ab eo lumine ueritatis.

146–148 *Feruebant...Albanum*: cf. Bede, *Historia* 1.7 (p. 28).
149 *lux tenebras*: cf. Io 1:5.
agnus lupos: cf. Lc 10:3.
152 *Verolamium*: Verulamium was a large city in Roman Britain, located in Hertfordshire, to the southwest of the present-day city of St. Albans.
158–159 *suscepit...mercede iusti*: Mt 10:41.
163–164 *Qui...accipit*: Io 13:20.
166–167 *donec...sue*: cf. Cant 3:4.
168 *Habitare...uestris*: Eph 3:17.
171 *Pascebat...eo*: cf. lines 64–65 above.

152 precepi : precipi *L* **162** Christiano : Christo *L* **171** eum : enim *L*

Christo, quem in eo susceperat, Martham et Mariam se pariter exhibebat. Martha erat satagendo circa frequens ministerium ut pasceret hospitem; Maria uero ex ore pii hospitis suauiter hauriendo ueritatem. Et quidem pius hospes signum fecit nullum, sed sacri eius mores pro signis fuere. Nec Albanus aliorum more incredulorum signa quesiuit aut signis indiguit, sed Christianos in hospite mores sagacissimus subtiliter contemplatus et pie admiratus est.

Deinde uoluit experiri quid in eius uerbis esset saporis, cuius mores tantum haberent dignitatis et decoris, sicque a contemplatione morum uentum est ad predicationem uerborum. Nam ut ait Apostolus, *Fides ex auditu, auditus autem per uerbum Christi.* Scriptum est de magistro celesti, quod cepit Ihesus facere et docere. Tenuit ille homo Dei formam dominicam: fecit et docuit. Prius predicauit Christum moribus, postea uerbis. Pro claritate signorum fuit ei insignis pietas morum. Magnus Iohannes, sicut scriptum est, signum fecit nullum, sed tanta erat gracia in illo morum sublimitas, ut Christus a multis putaretur. Sic et ille uir Dei signum quidem susceptori / *117va* suo nullum exhibuit, sed tanta in illo erat uite sinceritas ut ex ea ueri et summi Dei seruus agnosceretur. Itaque inchoata est eius predicatio pietate morum et consummata ueritate uerborum. Plantauit moribus, rigauit uerbis, de officio boni agricole nichil omittens. Verum neque qui plantat est aliquid, neque qui rigat, sed qui incrementum dat Deus. Frustra enim foris mores pollerent, uerba foris inaniter streperent, si non intus doceret qui docet hominem scientiam. Vnde nobis dicitur, *Vnus est enim magister uester qui in celis est.* Credidit ergo Albanus intus,

173–176 *Christo... ueritatem*: cf. Lc 10:38–42.
176–184 *Et... uerborum*: cf. Bede, *Historia* 1.7 (p. 28).
184–185 *Fides... Christi*: Rom 10:17.
185–186 *cepit... docere*: Act 1:1.
189–191 *Magnus... putaretur*: cf. Io 10:41–42.
190 *tanta... gracia*: an ablative of means, explaining the aetiology of John's *sublimitas morum*.
196–197 *neque qui plantat... Deus*: 1 Cor 3:7.
199-200 *Vnus... est*: cf. Mt 23:8–9.
200–203 *Credidit... uideret*: cf. Bede, *Historia* 1.7 (p. 28).

175 Maria *S* : Mariam *L* **188** ei *S* : eis *L* **198** si *S* : sed *L*

docente celesti magistro per ministerium predicatoris foris disserentis, et credendo eductus est de tenebris, redditus est luci, non qua statim luceret, sed per quam uideret.

Tunc primum uidit Albanus quod esset niger, immo nigerrimus, et cepit desiderare lauacrum quo dealbaretur et nomini suo aptaretur. Ventum est ad aquam salutis; intrauit et exiuit. Intrauit tenebrosus, exiuit lucidus; intrauit niger, exiuit albus. Tunc mutauit Ethiops pellem suam, et dedit pellem pro pelle, nigram pro nitida, tenebrosam pro lucida. Ethiops inquam ille qui dicebatur 'Albanus' mutata pelle factus est uere 'Albanus.' Factus est candidus, futurus post modicum eciam rubicundus. Factus est, inquam, in sacro baptismate candidus, sed non statim lilium. Denique post baptismum, exuberante gracia, cepit in uirtutibus crescere et proficiendo candescere usque ad candorem eximium, et sic factus est lilium, futurus mox rosa. Ante ergo lilium fuit quam rosa, quod quidem paucorum / *117vb* est, ut superius diximus. Quod autem non tantum in passione, sed et ante passionem fuerit lilium sanctitatis, post passionem futurus ex rosa lilium eterne iocunditatis, paucis insinuare libet.

Latebat adhuc apud ipsum pius ille ex hospite magister, et sacris eum colloquiis uel de fidei misteriis subtilius instruebat, uel ad martyrium animabat. Vbi uero sufficienter instructus eciam ad sustinenda pro Christo aduersa perfectum animi robur accepit, iam non ulterius sub pedagogo esse debuit. Quia ergo supernus prouisor et magistrum forte ad alia lucra, discipulum uero ad agonizandum uocabat Deo, uoluntatem suam bonam implendo per hominum uoluntatem malam, peruenit ad aures nefandi presidis quod penes Albanum lateret uir Dei, iussitque eum diligenter perquiri. Tum Albanus magistrum dimisit, ipsum quidem utilitati plurimorum seruare intendens, se autem passioni pro eo constanter exponens. Cedens ergo illi habitum

208 *mutauit...suam*: cf. Ier 13:23.

211 *Factus...rubicundus*: cf. Cant 5:10.

224 *iam...debuit*: cf. Gal 3:25.

227–229 *peruenit...perquiri*: cf. Bede, *Historia* 1.7 (p. 28). Here especially William borrows much of Bede's language. Bede writes, 'Peruenit ad aures nefandi principis confessorem Christi, cui necdum fuerat locus martyrii deputatus, penes Albanum latere; unde statim iussit milites eum diligentius inquirere.'

231–234 *Cedens...appareret*: cf. Bede, *Historia* 1.7 (p. 28).

suum in quo caucius fugeret, eius characalla induitur, in qua uel officialibus uel iudici ut manifestus Christianus insignius appareret. Ecce, quante uirtutis fuit et ante examen passionis, quam aptus martyrio et ante martyrium. Liquet igitur quod et ante passionis ruborem ad eximie creuerit sanctitatis nitorem. Lilium ergo fuit et antequam rosa esset, quod quidem paucorum prerogatiua est.

Sed queritur an se debuerit ingerere ad passionem, cum Dominus dicat, *Cum uos persecuti fuerint in hac ciuitate, fugite in aliam.* Cum enim eorum qui corpus occidunt nemo persequitur, occasionem fugere homo Dei non habet. Cum autem persecutor imminet ut occidat, fugiendum; sed ut comprehenderit, fortiter agendum est. Hanc nimirum regulam tenuit ille uir Dei, qui nostrum dealbauit Albanum. Persecutore seuiente, latuit quo/ad licuit. Fugit autem cum iam latere non potuit. Et *118ra*
certe Dominus dicit, *Perfectus omnis erit, si sit sicut magister eius.* Videtur ergo quod debuerit Albanus secundum preceptum Domini et exemplum magistri uel latere uel fugere, et non se ingerere ad passionem.

Ad quod dicimus quod pluribus ex causis homines Dei fugiunt eos qui corpus occidunt. Nam et qui latent quodammodo fugiunt. Denique ex fuga animi corpus latet, quia fugiens animus occasionem nactus corpus abscondit. Fugiunt quidam naturaliter horrendo mortem, ex illo affectu quo nemo unquam carnem suam odio habuit. Hunc affectum eciam ipse

232 *characalla*: 'long tunic.' William takes the term from Bede's narrative, and we are expected to understand that this particular tunic would identify Alban as a Christian cleric.

239 *Sed queritur*: on the *quaestio* form of the following section, see the Introduction, p. 20.

240–241 *Cum…aliam*: cf. Mt 10:23.

241–250 *Cum…passionem*: William clarifies the precept from Mt 10 that he has just quoted, proposing a counter-argument that questions the propriety of Alban's actions. He states that a man is only excused from fulfilling the Matthean precept when he is being sought out to be captured and not to be executed. Alban's confessor clearly adhered to this rule, because, sought out to be executed, he did flee. It appears, therefore, that Alban should have fled as well.

241 *qui…occidunt*: Mt 10:28, Lc 12:4.

243 *fugiendum*: supply *est* from line 244.

247–248 *Perfectus…eius*: cf. Lc 6:40.

Dominus et saluator noster secundum carnem in se habere atque exprimere dignatus est, *Pater*, inquiens, *si fieri potest, transeat a me calix iste*. Quidam eciam fugiunt ex consciencia uel metu proprie inbecillitatis, considerantes scilicet se minus habere in sumptibus, uel timentes ne forte non habeant sumptus idoneos, ad edificandam turrim magnam, id est martyrium subeundum.

Horum sane fuga atque illorum parum quidem laudabilis, plene tamen excusabilis est. Quidam autem fugiunt, ipsos persecutores propensius diligendo atque eis pie parcendo, ne habeant occasionem seuiendi crudelius, nolentes scilicet quantum in ipsis est cum aliorum detrimento preclaram mercedem adquirere. Hii plane laudabiliter fugiunt, sed illi laudabilius, qui altiori consideratione fugiendo se seruant ad lucra maiora atque utilitatem plurimorum. Sic fugit Paulus in sporta demissus.

Si autem comprehensus a persecutoribus homo Dei fugere non poterit, tunc nichil aliud quam fortiter in acie standum est, iuxta illud Psalmiste: *Viriliter agite et confortetur cor uestrum, omnes qui speratis in Domino*. Tunc secundum Iohelem / prophetam eciam, *Infirmus dicat quia, 'Fortis ego sum,'* sciens *118rb*
quod aderit Christus suis, et pro se agonizantibus subministrabit uires idoneas, ut et qui ante agonem defecate sanctitatis lilia non fuerant, in agone fiant. Et sciendum quod Dominus, cum dicit,

258–259 *Pater…iste*: cf. Mt 26:39.
261 *sumptibus*: 'resources.'
261–262 *uel…subeundum*: some people flee because they fear that they do not have the strength to endure martyrdom.
263–270 *Horum…demissus*: after enumerating the different reasons why a person might flee those who seek to kill him (lines 251–262), William states that Alban's confessor fled for the best possible reason, i.e. since he knew that he could better serve God by converting other pagans, as he had done with Alban.
270 *Sic…demissus*: cf. 2 Cor 11:33.
271–311 *Si…audacia*: William answers the question raised in lines 239–241, arguing that Alban was right not to flee. Instead of fulfilling the precept of Mt 10:23, Alban adhered to others that were more appropriate to him and, especially, to the fervor of his new-found Christianity. Cf. William's discussion of the woman in Lc 11:27, lines 73–91.
273–274 *Viriliter…Domino*: Ps 30:25.
275 *Infirmus…sum*: Ioel 3:10.
277 *defecate*: perfect passive participle, 'purified.'

Si uos persecuti fuerint in hac ciuitate, fugite in aliam, nulli fugam imperat, alioquin tot preclari martyres cum inobediencie reatu exissent. Persecutore inquam imminente nulli Dominus fugam imperat, sed uel concedit infirmis, uel fortibus consulit ad lucra maiora seruandis.

Porro Albanus quodam gracie priuilegio in breui tempora multa expleuerat, adhuc baptismate madidus ad insigne iam robur animi excreuerat, et perfecta caritate foras mittente timorem, amore martyrii fortiter ardebat. Nec fugiendum duxit spe lucri maioris, sed lucrum sacre mortis e proximo capessere uoluit. Itaque ad uictimam, immo uictoriam properans, futurus ideo uictor quia uictima, pro hospite ac magistro suo qui querebatur ad necem, funestis se satellitibus ultroneus optulit. Et quoniam nichil amplius quam misericordiam iudicis metuebat, in tali se habitu, per quem ille irritaretur, exibuit in utroque, id est in ultronea sui exibitione et in impii iudicis irritatione, summum martyrem, caput et formam martyrum preclare imitatus.

Nempe Saluator, appropinquante hora sacratissime passionis sue, tot prophetarum uocibus preclamate, tot sacrificiorum generibus et tot rerum enigmatibus presignate, ciuitatem triumpho suo nobilitandam ultro expetiit, et non simpliciter ut ante consueuerat, sed festiuus et gloriosus aduenit, cum tanta scilicet ac tali pompa per quam exulcerarentur atque in necem eius uehemencius concitarentur, quorum uoluntate et actione / tam mala subtili sapiencia usurus erat ad implendum *118va* propositum uoluntatis sue tam bone et tam pie. Itaque Albanus, pio spiritus feruore non imperatam a Domino sed concessam propter infirmitatem carnis detrectando fugam atque hilariter properando ad uictimam, nichil contra dominicum presumpsit imperium, sed Christiane fortitudinis quam in breui conceperat

279 *Si…aliam*: cf. Mt 10:23.
286–287 *perfecta…timorem*: cf. 1 Io 4:18.
293 *exibuit*: the scribe of Lambeth sometimes omits an 'h' from *exhibuit* and related words, though not uniformly: cf. line 192.
297–305 *Nempe…pie*: cf. Mt 21:8–9, Mc 11:8–10, Lc 19:36–38, Io 12:12–15.

294 ultronea *S* : utronea *L*

preclare celebrauit exordium. Optulit se propter Christum discrimini, sed pia fiducia, non presumptuosa uel precipiti audacia.

Exibetur a militibus presidi aris tunc forte assistenti atque immolanti demonibus. Quod utique diuinitus prouisum est, quo fortissimo martyri maior tribueretur uirtutis occasio atque insignior eius esset confessio. Impius enim iudex, funestis illis sacris specialiter intentus, in eorum contemptorem illo loco et illa sibi hora exibitum grauius erat seuiturus, ut quanto diis suis gracia loci et temporis uideretur esse deuotior, tanto eciam hostibus eorum, si qui tunc forte inciderent, infestior redderetur. Ad sustinendum ergo truculentiorem iudicis motum maiore animi uirtute opus fuit. Sed et illa hora atque illo loco, hoc est ubi et quando falsorum deorum pluralitas ritu sacrilego colebatur, insignius a nobili martyre unius ueri Dei reddenda erat confessio.

Inflammatur impius ad conspectum athlete fortissimi et exacuit ut gladium linguam suam, et cuius corpus gladio trucidaturus erat, animum eius gladio lingue prius sic ferit. 'Quia,' inquid, 'celare sacrilegum quam prodere maluisti, quecumque illi debebantur supplicia tu soluere habes, si a cultura deorum nostrorum temptas discedere.' Quibus uerbis rudi Christiano, quem ad mores pristinos facile reuocandum putabat, sic penas pro commisso de legis imperialis uigore intentat, / ut eciam *118vb* non discedenti a cultura demonum quasi de misericordia ueniam spondeat.

Falleris, O seua astucia uel fatua seuicia: noster enim Albanus non iam rudis sed fortis est Christianus. Etate quidem fidei rudis, sed non rudis eiusdem fidei uiribus. Quod paucorum priuilegium est, in tenera fidei etate solidum fidei robur habet. Reboat ergo ante aras erroris clara ueritatis confessio, attonitum

312–313 *Exhibetur…demonibus*: cf. Bede, *Historia* 1.7 (p. 30).
315-330 *Impius…discedere*: cf. Bede, *Historia* 1.7 (p. 30).
330–334 *Quibus…spondeat*: the judge threatens Alban in an attempt to scare him into proclaiming himself to be a pagan once again, rather than trying to win him over with any argument in favour of that religion.

315 funestis *S* : funestus *L* **335** astucia *S* : iusticia *L*

facit iudicem inusitate libertatis responsio. Miratur in nouitio nostro animum tam ingentem, et de uirtute stupidus percunctatur genus eius secundum carnem. Tenuit homo Dei regulam illam Salomonis: *Responde stulto secundum stulticiam suam.* Requisitus de carne, respondit de spiritu; requisitus de familia et genere, respondit de religione. Vir spiritualis eggregie dedignatus est homini carnali respondere de carne, iuxta illud uiri sapientis: *Cum uiro irreligioso tracta de sanctitate, et cum uiro iniusto de iusticia.*

Et forte non tantum ingenue mentis iudicio sed eciam pia quadam cautela sic respondit homini nichil preter carnem sapienti. Forte enim in genere eius tales erant persone, quarum gracia iudex illi parcendum decerneret. Quia ergo flagrans amore martyrii animus nichil maius quam iudicis clemenciam formidabat, idcirco, ut arbitror, subticendo genus suum misericordiam iudicis euitare, religionem quam susceperat libere proclamando furorem eius uehemencius uoluit concitare. Frustratus iudex in questione generis questionem facit nominis. Ille uero sciens nullum ex noticia nominis fore impedimentum passionis nomen indicat olim sibi inditum: 'Albanum ' se dicit a parentibus nominatum, consequenter insinuans Christiana se religione nomini suo aptatum, id est dealbatum a maculis nascendo et agendo contractis. Sane illud Dauiticum, / *Os iusti* *119ra* *meditabitur sapienciam, et lingua eius loquetur iudicium*, ante passionis examen excellenter in martyre nostro impletum est. In premissis siquidem responsionibus os eius insigniter meditatum est sapienciam. Porro in responsione subsequenti lingua eius preclare locuta est iudicium. Cum enim iudex sacris uerbis exasperatus ferocius immineret, acerbe illi mortis sed temporalis,

343 *Responde...suam*: Prov 26:5.
344–345 *requisitus...religione*: cf. Bede, *Historia* 1.7 (p. 30).
347–348 *Cum...iusticia*: Eccli 37:12.
354 *subticendo*: 'being silent.'
356–357 *Frustratus...nominis*: cf. Bede, *Historia* 1.7 (p. 30).
359–360 *Albanum...nominatum*: Bede, *Historia* 1.7 (p. 30).
362–363 *Os...iudicium*: Ps 36:30.
367–371 *Cum...ydolorum*: cf. Bede, *Historia* 1.7 (p. 30).

341–342 percunctatur *S* : percuncuntatur *L*

nisi sacrificaret ydolis, intentans supplicium, ille econtra penas gehennales et eternas sollempniter comminatus est cultoribus ydolorum.

Sed quid uerbis, iudex fatue, immoraris? Annon satis erat ex ore iusti audisse sapienciam? At, contemptor sapiencie, audisti eciam ex lingua eius iudicium. Nichil amplius ex ore iusti expectandum est, totum illud Dauiticum iam in eius responsionibus impletum est. Obsurduisti non tantum ad sapienciam que ex ore eius leniter sonuit, sed eciam ad iudicium quod ex lingua eius terribiliter tonuit, *Ergo quod facis, fac cicius*. Quem non terruerunt, non emollierunt uerba, habes examinare per uerbera. Ceditur martir a ministris presidis, plane immisericordius quam cesus est olim a Iudeis, accipiens scilicet quadragenas una minus. In modico pepercerunt Apostolo cedentes Iudei, eo quod nollent de crudelitate notari, at in nullo pepercerunt martyri nostro funesti carnifices, de sola misericordia a iudice culpari uerentes. Torquetur uero confessor eggregius penis acerrimis; patitur propter Christum insigniter, hoc est non tantum pacienter sed eciam gaudenter, eratque illi in mediis suppliciis sonus epulantis. Tam multa martyrum milia pro Christo fortiter occubuere, contenti uirtute paciencie et non supererogantes. Tam multos inuenis penas pro Christo fortiter tolerasse, paucos in mediis penis exultasse.

Illud quippe Dauiticum martyribus maxime conuenit: *Euntes ibant et flebant portantes manipulos suos*. At noster ille athleta ibat et gaudebat portans manipulos suos. / *119rb* Quod utique insigne paucorum est. Num alicubi scriptum reperies, 'Exultabunt

378 *Ergo…cicius*: Io 13:27
381 *cesus est*: supply *Paulus* or *Apostolus*. In 2 Cor 11, Paul describes himself receiving thirty-nine lashes on five different occasions. His punishment thus conformed to Deut 25:3, which stated that a man should not be whipped in excess of forty lashes.
381–382 *accipiens…minus*: cf. 2 Cor 11:24.
382–383 *In…notari*: cf. Act 21–22.
387–388 *sonus epulantis*: Ps 41:5.
392–393 *Euntes…suos*: Ps 125:6.

369 econtra *S* : contra *L* **372** Annon *S* : At non *L* **384–385** culpari uerentes *S* : uerentes culpari *L*

sancti in penis'? At scriptum est, *Exultabunt sancti in gloria.* Illa utique de qua dicitur, *Graciam et gloriam dabit Dominus.* Prius graciam, postea gloriam, id est graciam pro gracia. Euntes ibant et flebant sancti portantes manipulos suos. Quo ibant? Quo portabant manipulos iusticie? Certe ad gloriam: per graciam, id est uirtutem paciencie, ibant ad gloriam. Flentes ibant ad gloriam, exultaturi in gloria. At quidam martyres habundantiori gracia exultarunt in penis quasi in gloria. Sane quam mirum est hoc, tam et eximium. Non pertinet ad turbam martyrum, quia, ut dixi, insigne paucorum est. In hac preclara paucitate noster inuenitur Albanus, non contentus in penis habere pacienciam, sed excellenti uirtuti superaddens gaudium et leticiam.

Arbitror hoc non simpliciter eximium, sed inter eximia preeximium. Alia quippe necessaria sunt, alia eximia. Necessaria sunt sine quibus non potest esse salus. Eximia uero sunt sine quibus potest esse, sed cum quibus gloriosa est, salus. Necessaria iubentur, eximia uero monentur. Illa habent legem precepti, hec uero libertatem consilii. Vnde Apostolus unum de eximiis, id est uirginitatem, commendans, *De uirginibus*, inquid, *preceptum Domini non habeo, consilium autem do.* Et quidem precipuum inter eximia resque sublimis consilii est

396 *Exultabunt…gloria*: Ps 149:5.
397 *Illa*: i.e. *gloria*.
Graciam…Dominus: Ps 83:12.
398 *graciam pro gracia*: Io 1:16
398–399 *Euntes…suos*: cf. Ps 125:6.
404–408 *Non…leticiam*: Using similar terms, William describes Mary as the preeminent martyr: *Explanatio* 3:9–10 (p. 163–164).
409 *Arbitror*: on the *quaestio* form of the following section, see the Introduction, p. 20.
410–411 *Necessaria…salus*: Hrabanus Maurus, *Tractatus Hrabani supra Actus Apostolorum*. The discussion of necessary and extraordinary things that follows this quotation is based upon this unpublished commentary, apropos of Act 15:28. See Cambridge, University Library, MS Ee.3.51, fols 195–241, here fol. 230v. The commentary is listed in Stegmüller, no. 7063.
415–416 *De virginibus…do*: 1 Cor 7:25.

407 uirtuti : uirtute *LS*

sustinere pro Christo supplicia pacienter: quanto magis eciam gaudenter? Paciencia in suppliciis propter Christum illatis martyrium facit. Leticia uero iuncta paciencie martyrium nobilitat. Paciencia in suppliciis fortis est, etsi non sit hilaris. Nam et illi fortes sunt, qui cum fletu portant manipulos suos. Verum paciencia excellenter est fortis si est et hilaris, et tanto fortior, quanto hilarior.

Fortassis autem alicui uidebitur martyrium non esse de eximiis, eo quod magis esse uideatur res necessitatis quam libertatis, res precepti quam res consilii. Dum enim ecclesia pacem habet, de subeundo / martyrio non agitur, siue per preceptum *119va* siue per consilium. Persecutionis uero detonante procella, fuga conceditur Christanis, dicente Christo, *Si uos persecuti fuerint in hac ciuitate, fugite in aliam.* At fugere non ualentes siue eciam nolentes non simpliciter monentur sed eciam iubentur non timere eos qui occidunt corpus, id est mortem quam inferunt fortiter tolerare. Si enim simpliciter monerentur, martyrium minime res esset precepti, sed pure res consilii, et sic esset liberum positis in persecutione uel fortiter agere uel non fortiter agere, id est tolerare pro Christo supplicia uel non tolerare. Quod si nefas est sentire uel dicere, immo quia nefas est, martyrium numquam res libertatis est, sed semper res necessitatis. Ergo nec res consilii est, sed res precepti. Atque ita quod durum est dicere, non inter eximia numerandum uidetur.

Huic obiectioni taliter respondemus. Martyrium ita est eximium, ut sit eciam, sicut predictum est, inter eximia precipuum. Non enim de necessariis est, cum sine martyrio possit eciam esse preclara salus. Denique tam multi hinc exeunt portantes

425–441 *Fortassis…uidetur*: as above, William creates a counter-argument, suggesting that martyrdom should be counted among the 'necessary things' and not the 'extraordinary things.' When they are not able to flee, i.e. to adhere to the command of Mt 10:23, then Christians are commanded (*iubentur*), not simply advised (*non simpliciter monentur*), not to fear their death, as in Mt 10:28. Martyrdom would therefore appear to be among the necessary things.

427–428 *ecclesia…habet*: cf. Act 9:31.

430–431 *Si…aliam*: cf. Mt 10:23.

433 *non…corpus*: Mt 10:28.

434 tolerare *S* : tollerare *L*

secum perfecte iusticie manipulos sine martyrio. Si ergo martyrium pure, id est sine incidentibus, in sua natura consideres, plane res libertatis resque consilii est. Gracia uero temporis efficitur res precepti, atque eo ipso res necessitatis, sed ideo foris efficitur res felicissime necessitatis, quia in sua natura pure est res libertatis. Felicem prorsus necessitatem dixerim, per quam res tam excellens et tam sublime consilium prouenit et sine qua non prouenit. Non enim martyrium, nisi forte laxata significacione martyrium intelligas—martyrium inquam quod proprie martyrium dicitur—passim capessere non licet, sed tunc solummodo cum persecutor imminet. Optione siquidem a persecutore proposita uel Christum negandi uel / de uita periclitandi, in *119vb*
hanc felicem detrusus necessitatem homo Dei rite capescit martirium, eligendo scilicet de uita carnis periclitari, dum morte amarius iudicat ueram uitam inficiari.

Cum ergo sine martyrio possit esse salus, quandoque tamen talis articulus incidit, ut sine ipso non possit esse salus, fitque gracia temporis ut non possit esse salus, nisi sit preclara salus. In hoc casu martyrium est ad salutem necessarium, non tamen iccirco minus excellens et eximium. Sic eciam cetera eximia, res scilicet consilii et ob hoc eciam res libertatis, laudabiliter, id est non tantum salua sed eciam aucta eximietate sua, contingit fieri res precepti et ob hoc eciam res necessitatis. Verbi gracia: relinquere omnia propter Christum a nullo exigitur, quia non est res precepti sed res consilii, res libertatis. Similiter et castrare se propter regnum celorum, id est tenere celibatum. Cum

447 *incidentibus*: by considering martyrdom free from its 'accidents' or 'specific circumstances,' William is responding directly to the objection raised in lines 425–429. Rather than concluding that martyrdom is necessary because it is compelled by a certain historical situation, William asserts that it is extraordinary, since martyrdom is not something *sine quibus non potest esse salus* (lines 410–411).

448 *Gracia…temporis*: another reference to martyrdom considered in its historical circumstances, perhaps best translated 'sometimes.'

453–455 *Non…licet*: *non* appears to be repeated because of the two interjections (*nisi…intelligas; martyrium…dicitur*) which appear between the first negative adverb and the main verb.

467 *eximietate*: 'extraordinariness.'

470–471 *castrare…celorum*: cf. Mt 19:12.

467 eximietate *S* : exiemietate *L*

autem quis contentus non est utrumque uel alterum obseruare simpliciter et libere, sed ad hoc uel illud obseruandum se uoto astringet, iam ab eo exigitur preceptum quod ad eius antea pendebat arbitrium. Districte enim et sub intentatione gehennalis supplicii precipit Deus uota rationabilia non infringi. Sic ergo eximia, que iccirco eximia sunt quoniam ex sua natura res sunt consilii et libertatis, ex adiuncto contingit fieri imperii et necessitatis, laudabiliusque obseruantur uoluntaria necessitate quam simplici uoluntate. Denique laudabilis ista necessitas ea, quo minus eximia sint, minime decolorat, sed pocius ut crescant ad eximietatem sancit et ornat.

Nec martyrium, quod ut diximus inter eximia precipuum est, pro eo quod ex sui natura res sublimioris consilii est, illa per quam capessitur insignius commendatur. Quod si martyr non tantum fortiter acerbissimos pro Christo cruciatus sustineat, sed eciam pre uberi caritate atque interne suauitatis / magnitudine *120ra* exultet in penis quasi in epulis, nonne iam uirtus martyrii excreuit usque ad summum? Tante excellencie noster Albanus titulo refulgebat, cum non solum pacienter sed eciam gaudenter acerrima pro Christo supplicia perferebat. Sed inuictum athletam iam Christus ex agone ad triumphum uocabat; celum quoque diucius ciuem suum incolari non sustinens, eum iam urgencius flagitabat.

480–482 *Denique…ornat*: the subject of *decolorat* and *sancit et ornat* is *laudabilis ista necessitas*, while the object is *ea*, supplying *eximia* either from the subclause or from the subject of the preceding sentence.

483–485 *Nec…commendatur*: 'Nor is martyrdom, which as we said is outstanding among extraordinary things, since by its nature it is a thing of higher counsel, more excellently commended according to that [necessity] through which it is attained.' The antecedent of *illa* (line 484) appears to be *necessitas* (line 480). Since William will go on to state that how the martyr acts while being killed is of the utmost importance, this sentence appears to be an example of understatement, i.e. martyrdom is commended just as conspicuously by how it is undergone as it is by its status as a *res sublimioris consilii*.

492–493 *celum…sustinens*: 'no longer tolerating that his citizen should not dwell in heaven.'

488 quasi *S* : quam *L*

Seuiebat iudex impius, et seuiendo diuinis dispositionibus seruiebat ignarus. Miles non bonus regi regum militabat nesciens, atque ideo non remunerandus pro milicia sed pro malicia et seuicia puniendus. Qui nimirum ubi animum martyris non solum inuictum sed eciam inuincibilem comperit, circa eius immutationem ulterius laborare superfluum duxit, et quem non poterant saltem contristare nedum emollire supplicia, cicius eradendum putauit de terra. Diabolus siquidem per suos satellites id agit ut anime pocius trucidentur quam corpora. Si uero, iuxta uotum eius et operam, mortes non proueniunt animarum, saltem mortibus pascitur corporum. Iussus ergo uir Dei, membrum scilicet nobile pro suo capite, capitalem subire sententiam, ducebatur ad locum sanguine suo nobilitandum. Ducebatur, inquam, Albanus ad locum dealbationis sue, ubi scilicet stolam suam in sanguine agni dealbaturus, id est fuso pro omnibus sanguine agni proprium sanguinem refusurus erat. Ducebatur inuictus ad uictimam, ideo plane uictor, quia uictima, futurus.

Sane quantum illi esset mori lucrum, quam pretiosa in conspectu Domini mors eius, tribus signis insignibus, duobus scilicet sub ipsa morte, tertio in ipsa morte, declaratum est. Eunti enim ad mortem, quem immolationi eius predestinarat diuinitas, fluuius intermeans moram facturus uidebatur, ponte preoccupato a turbis, quas uel curiositas uel pietas ad sacre mortis eius spectaculum traxerat. Ille uero pre amore martyrii omnis tunc more impaciens, et ne forte aliquid per morulam illam reuitato, ut assolet, iudice innouaretur sollicite metuens,

505–507 *Iussus...sententiam*: as elsewhere in this sermon (cf. lines 22–23), the Church, or specifically the host of martyrs, is referred to as the members or limbs of a body, of which Christ is the head. Cf. the similar discussion in the homily on Lc 11, lines 543–549. The juxtaposition of *capite* (referring to Christ) and *capitalem...sententiam* ('capital punishment') is suggestive of a pun.

509 *stolam...dealbaturus*: cf. Apoc 7:14.

513 *mori lucrum*: Phil 1:21.

513–514 *pretiosa...eius*: cf. Ps 115:15.

515–519 *Eunti...traxerat*: cf. Bede, *Historia* 1.7 (pp 30–32).

510 sanguine : sanguini *LS*

ad instar Helye, in spiritu et uirtute Helye, ad transitus sui obsequium siccauit fluminis alueum. Locum sue neci destinatum concitus adiit, ibi quidem pretiosum recentis / miraculi fructum *120rb* messurus, sed nequaquam ibi ut impio iudici placuerat moriturus. Deus enim uolebat eum in monte mori, ut non posset abscondi ciuitas super montem posita.

Adest spiculator, immo non iam spiculator sed diuine uirtutis in facto miraculo pius speculator. Lupus in agnum mira mutatione dextere excelsi repente conuertitur: ferrum quod in necem martyris de mandato iudicis sumpserat abiciens, gladio spiritus quod est uerbum Dei nouicius Christi miles accingitur, et iuxta formam apostolicam corde credens ad iusticiam, ore autem confitens ad salutem, martyri conmartyr adiungitur. Turbantur funesti satellites, tum pro contemplatione miraculi, tum pro subita mutatione conministri; ferrum quod ille proiecerat uelud candens cunctantur attingere, uerentes singuli pondus sanguinis iusti super se tollere. At inuentus est inter eos alter Doech, ausus forte dicere, 'Sanguis eius super me, et super oculos meos,' mortem quidem illaturus, sed mortuum non uisurus.

Illis ita cunctantibus martyr non substitit, sed ad locum quem in montis edito predestinarat ei Deus, comitantibus turbis, ascendit. Ibi dum sacre mortis flagrans desiderio spiculatorem prestolatur, uirtus ex ipso egreditur, signo priori aliud non minus insigne adiciens. Qui enim aquam in flumine dum transiret non reliquerat, potenti oratione aquam uiuam ex matrice abysso repente in aridum montis uerticem euocat. Ad uocatum uerbumque martiris ex inaquoso fons uiuus exoritur, ut ad eius obsequium recessisse fluuius comprobetur.

522–523 *ad instar...alueum*: cf. 4 Reg 2:8.
526–527 *non...posita*: cf. Mt 5:14.
528–534 *Adest...adiungitur*: cf. Bede, *Historia* 1.7 (p. 32).
528 *spiculator*: 'executioner.'
533–534 *corde...salutem*: cf. Rom 10:10.
538–539 *alter Doech*: cf. 1 Sam 22:17–18. Doech, or Doeg, was an Edomite herdsman who killed eighty-five priests, including the high priest Achimelech, at the command of Saul, when Saul's own court officials refused to carry out the executions.
546–547 *potenti...euocat*: cf. Bede, *Historia* 1.7 (p. 32).

541 cunctantibus *S* : cuntantibus *L* **542** comitantibus *S* : commitantibus *L*

Accedit truculentus spiculator, uidet unde inuidet, ustus grauiter claritate miraculi. Duobus signis tam insignibus non compungitur tercio proinde feriendus. Eximit mundo inferendum celo, nec ad punctum de scelere gauisurus. Faciens enim in martyre diuisionem capitis atque membrorum, in se ipso mox pertulit diuisionem capitis et oculorum: denique exilientes oculi illi nequam de capite una cum beati martyris capite deciderunt in terram. Tercium hoc signum fuit ad declarandum morientis meritum. Nam duo signa precedencia insignem / fecerant *120va* moriturum.

Peracta uictima, uictor in stola sua formosus, id est candidus et rubicundus, de ergastulo carnis egreditur, ab amicis angelis ilico excipitur, et suo regi triumphans miles, suo capiti membrum eximium sollempniter exhibetur. Ibi ab omnibus regem in decore suo uidentibus preclare salutatur, et mane nobiscum illi ab omnibus cum ingenti gaudio acclamatur. Fortissimum militem ex prelio uenientem uultu et uoce rex pius exhilarat: Euge, inquiens, serue bone et strenue: quia fortis fuisti in prelio, gloriosus eris in palatio. Intra nunc in gaudium Domini tui, qui et in suppliciis gauisus es pro Domino tuo. Inebriare nunc ab ubertate domus mee, et torrente uoluptatis mee potare, qui uino caritatis mee ebrius lusisti in tormentis uelut in epulis.

Sane et hoc beatissimi martyris nostri ornat triumphum, quod non solus hinc exiit, nec incomitatus ad Christum iit. Ereptam quippe nuper predam secum abduxit, et ex funesto carnifice pium iam confessorem, ex spina scilicet seuie rosam martyrii, pro magno et preclaro munere maiestatis uultibus presentauit. Et ei quidem, pro articulo temporis, aqua defuit ad baptismum, sed non defuit sanguis ad martyrium: uicem in eo sacri baptismatis impleuere confessio et sanguis. Qui enim ait,

553–557 *Faciens...terram*: cf. Bede, *Historia* 1.7 (p. 32).
560 *in...formosus*: Is 63:1.
560–561 *candidus...rubicundus*: Cant 5:10.
563–564 *regem...uidentibus*: cf. Is 33:17.
567–569 *Euge...tuo*: cf. Mt 25:21, 25:23.
569–571 *Inebriare...potare*: cf. Ps 35:9.
573–579 *Sane...martyrium*: cf. Bede, *Historia* 1.7 (p. 34).

574 incomitatus *S* : incommitatus *L*

Nisi quis renatus fuerit ex aqua et Spiritu Sancto, non potest introire in regnum Dei, ab hac una sententia confessores suos et martyres duabus aliis sentenciis exceptos tutosque facit, *Omnis*, inquiens, *qui confitebitur me coram hominibus, confitebor et ego eum coram Patre meo*, et, *Qui perdiderit animam suam propter me, in uitam eternam custodit eam.*

Et certe pluribus esse dinoscitur sanguis passionis quam aqua baptismatis. Facit enim ille quod illa, plenam scilicet remissionem peccatorum, sed habundat in effectu plurimum, quia aliis eciam meritis non extantibus solus computatur pro ubertate meritorum. Fusus ergo pro Christo sanguis non simpliciter implet, cum res ita poscit, uicem expiatricis aque, sed eciam habundat / ad conferendum priuilegium gracie. *120vb* Itaque homo ille, ex lupo seuicie in agnum innocencie repente conuersus, cum pro temporis angustia salientis aqua deesset, titulo confessionis insignis in sanguine suo melius baptizatus est, et hoc apte satis. Decebat enim hominem sanguinarium in sanguine pocius quam in aqua baptizari. Nullus alius, ut reor, ad tante glorie celsitudinem compendio breuiore peruenit. Nam paulo ante uir sanguinum truculentus carnifex, atque inter alios carnifices palmam crudelitatis tenens, repente clarus titulo confessionis et rubens sanguine passionis ad regnum celeste quodammodo rapitur, et martyrum numero sociatur.

Hunc noster Albanus ad locum properans passionis fuerat paulo ante lucratus, et hic illi pergenti ad Christum indiuiduus comes est datus. Qui nimirum ante suum lucratorem occubuit, si unum uterque carnificem pertulit. Sed credibilius est quod uno momento occubuerint diuersos experti carnifices, ut pariter exeuntes ad Christum pariter ducibus angelis properarent. Qui enim uenerabili Albano necem intulit, in ipso ictu simul cum oculis carnificis officium perdidit. Sed et alii qui aderant carnifices, exemplum uerentes, diriguere. Nam et ferocissimi iudicis

581–582 *Nisi...Dei*: Io 3:5.
583–585 *Omnis...meo*: Mt 10:32.
585–586 *Qui...me*: Mt 10:39; cf. Lc 9:24.
586 *in...eam*: Io 12:25.
595 *salientis*: 'fountain.'
612–614 *Nam...putauit*: cf. Bede, *Historia* 1.7 (p. 34).

587 pluribus : plurimis *LS* **589** effectu : affectu LS **591** sanguis *S* : sanguinis *L* **602** rubens *S* : rubes *L*

animus signorum claritate perstrictus elanguit et nichil ulterius aduersus pios audendum putauit. Sic martyr magnificus a morte plurimos moriendo exemit, et, dato proprii sanguinis pretio, laboranti ecclesie pacem redemit. Seuiit hostilis gladius usque ad ipsum, post ipsum minime, eius scilicet sanguine hebetatus atque retunsus. Pacem in ecclesia non inuenerat, sed pacem hinc abiens ecclesie reliquit: pacem suam bonus filius pie matri dedit. Plane suam, quia sanguine suo fortiter adquisitam.

O uirum uirtutis precipue! O nostre preclarissimam lampadem insule! Insigniuit uictoriis et meritis martyrum propicia diuinitas orbem terrarum, nec toto seclusos orbe Britannos deseruit, quibus Albanum donauit. Habent singule orbis prouincie lumina sua gaudentque / singulis patronis propriis; nostra extra *121ra* orbem per Albanum insula eximie dealbatur et de tanto patrono propensius gloriatur. Qui nimirum insigne est testimonium gracie largioris, scilicet quod non sit contenta superna pietas orbem terrarum uisitare, sed et extra orbem se porrigens occeanum quoque dignata sit penetrare. Denique uersificator egregius, Fortunatum dico, cum illustriores electos describeret, qui sua uel uita uel morte nobilitarunt orbem terrarum, contemplando progrediens eciam extra orbem, id est in ipso occeano, aduertit insignia gracie et titulos sanctitatis, atque unde potissimum nobilitaretur occeanus, metrica suauitate et subtili breuitate aperiens, 'Albanum,' inquid, 'egregium fecunda Britannia profert.' Fecunda plane Britannia fructu multiplici, sed fructus eius precipuus Albanus egregius.

Celebratur Britannia uariarum generatione specierum, atque inter cetera in aquilonali sui parte gemmas gignit candidas, quas dicimus uniones uel margaritas. Verum in ea nichil sic eminet,

636–637 *Albanum...profert*: Venantius Fortunatus, *De virginitate*, line 155 (PL 88:270c). William appears to have taken this quotation from Bede, *Historia* 1.7 (p. 28): both historians modify the word order of the verse, which in the original reads, 'Egregium Albanum fecunda Britannia profert.'

640–641 *in...margaritas*: cf. Bede, *Historia* 1.1 (p. 14). William follows Bede's account in praising pearls (*uniones uel margaritas*) as a beautiful natural resource of the north of Britain; Alban, however, is the most precious pearl of the south.

619 reliquit *S* : reliquid *L* **629** uisitare *S* : uisita *L*

nichil sic candet, ut illa una in australi eius parte margarita pretiosa, quam ob graciam candoris eximii Albanum superna uoluit pietas nominari. Felix Britannia, si datis omnibus suis comparasset eam, nunc autem felicior, quia gemmam propriam qua perpetuo decoretur atque preluceat minime comparauit, sed ex se pocius generauit, largiente bonorum omnium largitore Deo et Domino nostro Ihesu Christo, qui cum Patre et Spiritu Sancto uiuit et regnat per omnia secula seculorum. Amen.

642–643 *margarita pretiosa*: Mt 13:46.

INDEX OF SCRIPTURAL REFERENCES

In the following, roman numerals refer to the number of the sermon (I Sermo de Trinitate pp 38–57, II Cum loqueretur Ihesus ad turbas pp 61–83, III De Sancto Albano pp 87–110), while arabic numerals refer to the line numbers within the sermon.

TORONTO MEDIEVAL LATIN TEXTS

1 *Three Lives of English Saints*, ed. Michael Winterbottom (1972)
2 *The Gospel of Nicodemus*, ed. H.C. Kim (1973)
3 *Peter the Venerable: Selected Letters*, ed. Janet Martin (1974)
4 *A Thirteenth-Century Anthology of Rhetorical Poems*, ed. Bruce Harbert (1975)
5 *Two Alcuin Letter-Books*, ed. Colin Chase (1975)
6 *Three Latin Comedies*, ed. Keith Bate (1976)
7 *The Life of Gundulf, Bishop of Rochester*, ed. Rodney Thomson (1977)
8 *Boccaccio: In Defence of Poetry. Genealogiae deorum gentilium liber XIV*, ed. Jeremiah Reedy (1978)
9 *Bartholomaeus Anglicus: On the Properties of Soul and Body. De proprietatibus rerum libri III et IV*, ed. R. James Long (1979)
10 *Selected Sermons of Stephen Langton*, ed. Phyllis B. Roberts (1980)
11 *Philippe de Mézières' Campaign for the Feast of Mary's Presentation*, ed. William E. Coleman (1981)
12 *The Canterbury Hymnal*, ed. Gernot R. Wieland (1982)
13 *The Rule of St Benedict: The Abingdon Copy*, ed. John Chamberlin (1982)
14 *Robert Grosseteste: Templum Dei*, ed. Joseph Goering and F.A.C. Mantello (1984)
15 *The Oxford Poems of Hugh Primas and the Arundel Lyrics*, ed. C.J. McDonough (1984)
16 *Avitus: The Fall of Man. De spiritalis historiae gestis libri I-III*, ed. Daniel J. Nodes (1985)
17 *Nigel of Canterbury: Miracles of the Virgin Mary, in verse. Miracula sancte Dei genitricis virginis Marie, versifice*, ed. Jan Ziolkowski (1986)
18 *A Durham Book of Devotions*, ed. Thomas H. Bestul (1987)
19 *Speeches from the Oculus pastoralis*, ed. Terence O. Tunberg (1990)

20 *The 'Vulgate' Commentary on Ovid's Metamorphoses: The Creation Myth and the Story of Orpheus*, ed. Frank T. Coulson (1991)
21 *Richard Rolle: Emendatio vitae; Orationes ad honorem nominis Ihesu*, ed. Nicholas Watson (1995)
22 *Latin Colloquies from Pre-Conquest Britain*, ed. Scott Gwara (1996)
23 *Stella clericorum*, ed. Eric H. Reiter (1997)
24 *Fra Nicola da Milano: Collationes de beata virgine*, ed. M. Michèle Mulchahey (1997)
25 *The Fables of 'Walter of England,'* ed. Aaron E. Wright (1997)
26 *A Book of British Kings: 1200 BC–1399 AD*, ed. A.G. Rigg (2000)
27 *Saints' Lives by Walter of Châtillon: Brendan, Alexis, Thomas Becket*, ed. Carsten Wollin (2002)
28 *The Ancestry of Jesus: Excerpts from Liber generationis Iesu Christi filii Dauid filii Abraham (Matthew 1:1–17)*, ed. Greti Dinkova-Bruun (2005)
29 *The Deposition of Richard II: 'The Record and Process of the Renunciation and Deposition of Richard II' (1399) and Related Writings*, ed. David R. Carlson (2007)
30 *An Epitome of Biblical History: Glosses on Walter of Châtillon's Alexandreis 4.176–274*, ed. David Townsend (2008)
31 *The Sermons of William of Newburgh*, ed. A.B. Kraebel (2009)